a place to live

Also by

NATALIA GINZBURG

The Road to the City

All Our Yesterdays

The Things We Used to Say

The Little Virtues

Valentino *and* Sagittarius, *two novellas*

No Way

The Manzoni Family

Family *and* Borghesia, *two novellas*

Voices in the Evening

The City and the House

a place to live

and other selected essays of

NATALIA GINZBURG

Chosen and translated by

LYNNE SHARON SCHWARTZ

Seven Stories Press

NEW YORK | LONDON | TORONTO | SYDNEY

Seven Stories Press
140 Watts Street
New York, NY 10013
www.sevenstories.com

In Canada: Hushion House, 36 Northline Road, Toronto, Ontario M4B 3E2

In the U.K.: Turnaround Publisher Services Ltd., Unit 3, Olympia Trading Estate,
Coburg Road, Wood Green, London N22 6TZ

In Australia: Tower Books, 2/17 Rodborough Road, Frenchs Forest NSW 2086

Library of Congress Cataloging-in-Publication Data
Ginzburg, Natalia.
    [Essays. English. Selections]
    A place to live : and other selected essays of Natalia Ginzburg / Natalia
Ginzburg ; chosen and translated by Lynne Sharon Schwartz.
        p. cm.
    ISBN 1-58322-474-2 (Cloth)
    1. Ginzburg, Natalia–Translations into English.   I. Schwartz, Lynne Sharon.
II. Title.
    PQ4817.I5 A27 2002
    854'.912–dc21   2002001559

9 8 7 6 5 4 3 2 1

College professors may order examination copies of Seven Stories Press titles for a
free six-month trial period. To order, visit www.sevenstories.com/textbook, or fax on
school letterhead to (212) 226-1411.

Book design by Cindy LaBreacht
Printed in the U.S.A.

contents

[5]

III

FROM *Vita immaginaria,* 1974

IV

SELECTIONS FROM *Serena Cruz o la vera giustizia,* 1990

preface

Natalia Ginzburg's essays require no explication. The opposite of hermetic, they are startlingly direct, forthright, and thorough. They leave readers stunned with recognition, fixed on the inexorable paths the sentences have cleared. The limpid ease of the language seems at odds with the author's pungent accounts of the labor and struggle the writing demanded. But of course she struggled: it is no small task to write so simply yet have each page radiant with allusion, brimming with what has grown between the lines.

The essays show a sensibility laid bare. Apart from the impeccable style, a nakedness of thought and emotion—of the contours and dynamics of thought and emotion—is their most arresting quality. Ginzburg delivers the genesis, the embryonic growth, and the full flowering of an idea or sensation as if it were a rare and gleaming mutation from the ordinary. But a reader may want a few facts as well.

Born in 1916, Ginzburg grew up in Turin in a large and volatile family closely connected to prominent intellectuals and artists; their domestic life is unforgettably portrayed in her 1963 autobiographical novel, *Family Sayings* (recently reissued under the less apt title, *The Things We Used to Say*). The tempestuous father who appears in several of the essays was a professor of anatomy and a non-observant Jew. During the 1920's and '30's, as fascism was taking hold, the family and its circle were actively anti-fascist, and the sense of alienation and combativeness Ginzburg knew in her youth pervades her essays and many novels. She began writing as a child, as she relates with her customary wry self-scrutiny in "My Craft" and "Fantasy Life," and published her first story at seventeen.

In 1938 she married Leone Ginzburg (their early days to-gether are memorably sketched in "Human Relations"). During their years of political exile in the village poignantly described in "Winter in the Abruzzi," Ginzburg wrote her first novel, *The Road to the City* (published in 1942 under a pseudonym because of the racial laws proscribing the rights of Jews). After their re-turn to Rome, Leone Ginzburg was arrested and died in prison at the hands of the fascists in 1944. Left on her own with three children, Ginzburg lived first in Rome, in the state of mind evoked in "My Psychoanalysis" and "Laziness," then returned to Turin and continued working with the group of writers who formed Einaudi, soon to become Italy's most distinguished pub-lishing house. In 1950 she married Gabriele Baldini, a professor of English literature, and lived with him in Rome until his death in 1969. (It was through Baldini's work that she spent time in England and came to write "The Great Lady," about her discov-ery of Ivy Compton-Burnett's novels.)

Ginzburg's death in 1991 was the occasion for an outpouring of critical praise and affectionate personal reminiscence in the Italian press. In her native country she has long been recog-nized as one of its greatest twentieth-century writers, and the most eloquent, incisive, and provocative chronicler of the war years and the postwar ambience (notably in *All Our Yesterdays* and *Voices in the Evening*). Mostly what she provoked was love and allegiance, but there was occasional exasperation at the outspoken, intransigent quality of her thought and moral judgments (precisely what I find most endearing). The critic Enzo Siciliano, while expressing awe for Ginzburg's "grasping things without any intellectual filters," also notes that this "very peremptory and direct way of presenting her ideas" could alienate readers accustomed to a more temperate mode of argument.

Despite the disingenuously modest stance of several of the essays ("I don't know anything about politics," for example, as the opening of the astute "An Invisible Government"), hers was a life spent at the center of Italian culture; she even served for one term in Parliament. She enjoyed a close circle of literary friends whose work she did not hesitate to criticize sternly when she saw fit—Alberto Moravia, for one, or Giulio Einaudi, as evidenced in "No Fairies, No Wizards."

Though the trauma and grief of Leone Ginzburg's death colored her life and work forever, Ginzburg remained unremittingly dedicated to her craft and to speaking out against injustice and equivocation. Her novels and plays focus on large moral issues as played out ruefully, often with tragicomic results, in the lives of individual characters. But the essays are where she speaks in her most candid voice. It is the intimate yet elusive tone of that voice, along with the challenge of trying to hear it in English, that has long intrigued me.

I first encountered her work back in the 1960's, during a crash course in intermediate Italian at the *Università per stranieri* (University for Foreigners) in Perugia. The professor believed in instant immersion and set us to reading Ginzburg's essays because of their extremely simple, straightforward language (although the simple passages are punctuated with sudden bursts of syntactical convolution). I was delighted, first, that I could understand them with my rudimentary Italian. I found their author magisterial and wise but accessible, full of indignation, sly wit, homely details. As I read on and learned more about her, I realized that the surface lucidity concealed a complex, passionate mind, fully invested in every sentence. Out of the banalities of daily life, she was weaving a web of moral and philosophical subtlety and paradox.

The pleasure of her contradictions seduced me, as well as the rigor of her thinking: a stubborn, unsparing gaze informed by vast compassion; humor that flashed forth brilliantly and unexpectedly—in a writer whose favorite subjects were contemporary anomie, moral failure, and war and its grievous aftermath; above all, the elaborations that turned up like sinuous detours, after the trusting traveler has been expecting a straight, easy road. At some point on this mesmerizing journey it is apparent that we've been led into darker and denser territory than we bargained for. Ginzburg forces us to examine the smallest and largest aspects of our lives with a daunting yet energizing scrutiny. By the end of each essay layered with subversive thought and feeling, we have to marvel at how she has managed to bring us so far, and so fast.

I began translating her essays those many years ago, not only as a way to learn Italian but as an inspiration for my own writing, and as a way to keep that heartbreaking, uncompromising voice close by. It happened, back then, that a friend arranged for me to meet Ginzburg in the apartment described in "A Place to Live." I didn't know what I would say, but couldn't resist the chance to be in the same room with the writer who so entranced me; even her suffering, I regret to say, gave her a kind of glamor in my eyes. The meeting was not a great success. We drank tea in a darkish living room. She sat very straight; she wore dark clothes; she was austere, unsmiling, civil but not helpful. She seemed puzzled about what I wanted of her, which was reasonable, seeing as I myself didn't quite know. We talked for a constrained hour and I was glad when it was over. Afterwards I thought there must be a way to talk to a famous author that I had yet to learn. I did learn, that day, that the author we love on the page is not the same person we meet in a living room. Nevertheless, the austerity and unwavering sense of self were the embodiment of what I had found in her books.

Some years later I reviewed her novel *No Way* (*Caro Michele* in the Italian edition) for *The Nation.* The review somehow found its way to her (not by my doing) and she wrote me a warm, appreciative letter. I was pretty sure she didn't connect the reviewer with the young person who had sat, awkward and near-speechless, in her living room. Still, I felt happily relieved, as if I had redeemed myself in her sight.

Now, when the work I began over thirty years ago is done, that personal encounter no longer matters to me. With literature, the past consumes the personal and circumstantial and leaves the essential, which is the work, the words. In the case of Ginzburg, their particular power is in delineating how intricate are our responses to ordinary and extraordinary events, how fraught with dread and absurdity and effort is that "long and inevitable parabola...we have to travel to feel, at last, a bit of compassion." Every inch of that parabola is traced with rigorous, ardent clarity. Each Ginzburg sentence reminds us that everything we say and do matters too much for carelessness and evasion. This makes daily life more difficult, yes, but more charged and exhilarating too.

If what Ginzburg offers in her essays is the examined life, then the acuity of her writing is in the process of examination. It has been a privilege to witness and partake of that process.

the little virtues, Ginzburg's first collection of essays, was published by Einaudi in 1963. In the selections included here, Ginzburg begins her ruminations on the themes that will occupy her entire life: the spiritual and moral devastation of the war, the writer's craft, and the vast, amorphous, and compelling subject she calls "Human Relations."

Typically, and deliberately, the essays tell a great deal about Ginzburg's feelings and attitudes but give few facts. The "right person" who appears in "Human Relations" was Leone Ginzburg, the professor of Russian literature and avid anti-fascist whom the author married in 1938. As a result of his political activities the couple and their young children were exiled to the village described in "Winter in the Abruzzi," achingly recalled as "the best time of my life." "The Son of Man" was written in 1946, just after the war, and less than two years after Leone Ginzburg was arrested and killed by the fascists. The agonies Ginzburg lights on so briefly but wrenchingly are literal, not metaphorical; the harshness of her adherence to truth rises from the sour fruit of experience, and will flavor the rest of her life and work.

"My Craft" is her first long brooding about the genesis and nature of her own writing, and should be read alongside later essays on the same theme: "Portrait of a Writer" and "Fantasy Life." Taken together, the three form a kaleidoscopic image of Ginzburg's self-examination at different stages in her writing life.

The style matures, the emphasis changes, but the unique voice, the wit, the utter devotion and the intensity remain the same.

(A curious footnote about this essay's title turns up in a recent book transcribing a series of 1990 radio interviews with Ginzburg—*E difficile parlare di sé* [*It's Hard to Talk About Oneself*], Einaudi, 1999.) She mentions that her good friend and severe critic, novelist Elsa Morante, didn't like the essay or the title. "She said it wasn't a craft, 'craft' was a word she rejected. In general she didn't like my essays, those pieces that, I don't know, I call essays...." The interviewer asks whether Morante found the word "craft" too prosaic. "I don't know," Ginzburg says. "It didn't appeal to her, she said it wasn't the right word. I left it anyway, it seemed to me it was.... It was the word that had first occurred to me, and I got attached to it.")

Like the theme of craft, the account of Ginzburg's childhood and family in "Human Relations" is also echoed later on, in a different mood, namely in "The White Mustache" and "Summer." For a more detailed and dazzling depiction of Ginzburg's early years in an atypical and chaotic family, her autobiographical novel, *The Things We Used to Say*, is indispensable.

human relations

A t the center of our life is the question of human relations: as soon as we become aware of it, that is, as soon as it presents itself as a distinct question rather than a baffling ache, we begin reconstructing its history and retracing its long path through our life.

In childhood we focus primarily on the world of adults, which we find dark and mysterious. It seems absurd, because we cannot grasp what the adults are saying to each other, nor the meaning of their actions and decisions or the reasons for their changes of mood, their sudden fits of rage. We cannot grasp what the adults are saying and we're not interested, indeed we find it infinitely tedious. What does interest us are their decisions, which can alter the course of our days, their dark moods that cast a pall over lunches and dinners, the sudden slamming of doors and outbursts of voices in the night. We have learned that a calm conversation can erupt at any moment into an unexpected storm, with the sounds of doors slamming and objects being hurled. We're anxiously on the alert for the slightest edge of violence in their voices. We might be absorbed in some game all by ourselves, and with no warning, angry voices rip through the house; mechanically, we go on playing, sticking stones and grass into a little pile of dirt to make a hill, but the hill doesn't really matter anymore, we can't be happy until peace returns to the house; doors slam and we jump; furious words fly from room to room, incomprehensible words; we don't seek to understand them or decipher what murky reasons gave rise to them; in our bewilderment we assume they must be dreadful reasons. The whole absurd mystery of adults bears down on us. Very often it complicates our relationships in the world of our peers, with children: very often a friend has come over to play, we're making a hill together, and a slammed door signals that peace is over; burning with shame, we pretend to be totally caught up in making the hill, we struggle to distract our friend from those savage voices resounding through the house; we carefully stick little pieces of wood into the mound of dirt, our hands suddenly grown limp and flaccid. We're quite certain there's no fighting in our friend's house, no voices yelling wild words; in our friend's house everyone is calm and civilized; fighting is a disgrace peculiar to our house. Then one day to our great relief we discover that they fight in our friend's house just the same as in ours; maybe they fight in every house on earth.

We've come into adolescence when the words adults speak become intelligible—intelligible but unimportant, since we no longer care whether or not there's peace in the house. We can follow the thread of domestic quarrels now, foresee their course and duration: they no longer frighten us. Doors slam and we don't jump; home is not what it once was—it's no longer our vantage point on the rest of the universe, just a place where we happen to live and eat our meals. We eat in haste, distracted, barely listening to what the adults are saying, their intelligible but pointless words. We eat and dash off to our room so as not to hear all their pointless words; we can be quite content even if the adults around us are fighting and sulking for days on end. What matters to us no longer takes place within the walls of our

house but outside, on the street and at school: we can't be happy
if our classmates look down on us ever so slightly. We would do
anything to save ourselves from their scorn, anything at all. We
write comic verses to make our classmates laugh, and recite
them with funny grimaces we're ashamed of later; to win their
regard we collect dirty words; we hunt for dirty words all day
long in books and dictionaries at home; we notice that our classmates have taken to dressing in a loud, flashy way, and so we too,
against our mother's will, take pains to insinuate some flashy
and vulgar touches in our sober clothes. We have the vague
sense that they must scorn us above all because of our shyness.
Who knows, maybe it was that far-off moment when we were
making mudpies with our friend—the doors slamming, the savage voices resounding, the shame burning our cheeks—that
very moment when shyness took root in us. We think we'll be
spending our whole life freeing ourselves from shyness, learning to move under the gaze of others with the same confidence
and nonchalance as when we're alone. Our shyness seems the
most serious obstacle to gaining love and universal approval,
and we're hungry and thirsty for this approval. In our solitary
fantasies, we ride triumphantly through the city on horseback,
surrounded by a cheering, adoring crowd.

At home, we punish the adults, whose absurd mystery bore
down on us for so many years, by our profound contempt, our
silence, our impenetrable face; for years we were obsessed by
their mystery, and now we avenge it with our own mystery, a
mute, impenetrable face and eyes of stone. We even take re-
venge on the adults at home for our schoolmates' scorn, a scorn
that seems aimed not only at us personally but at our whole
family, our social standing, all our furnishings and household
goods, our parents' manners and way of life. Every now and
then the old familiar rage breaks out at home, sometimes even

provoked by us, by our stony face. We're assaulted by a flurry of furious words; doors slam but we don't jump; now the doors are slamming on our account, while we sit motionless at the table with a haughty smile. Later, alone in our room, this haughty smile will instantly dissolve and we'll burst into tears, wallowing in our isolation and at being universally misunderstood, and we'll take a strange pleasure in shedding those scorching tears, stifling our sobs in a pillow. Soon our mother comes in, she's moved at the sight of our tears and invites us out for ice cream or a movie; with swollen, red eyes but a face once more stony and impenetrable, we sit next to our mother at a café table eating ice cream in tiny spoonfuls. All around us is a buzzing crowd of serene, cheerful people, while we and we alone are the most bleak, ungainly, loathsome creature that ever lived.

Who are others and who are we? we wonder. Sometimes we spend the whole afternoon alone in our room, lost in thought, wondering, with a slight sense of giddiness, if other people really exist or if we ourselves are inventing them. Maybe in our absence everyone else ceases to exist, vanishes in a flash, to be miraculously reborn, springing forth from the earth the moment we turn around. What if one day we turned around very suddenly and saw nothing and no one, we were just peering out into the void? In that case, we decide, there's no need to get so unhappy over the scorn of others; if those others don't exist, then they can't be thinking anything, either about us or about themselves. In the midst of these giddy notions, our mother comes to invite us out for ice cream, and we feel unaccountably, inordinately happy at the thought of the ice cream we'll soon be eating. Why such happiness at the prospect of ice cream, we wonder, we who are so grown up with our giddy thoughts, so weirdly lost in a world of shadows? We accept our mother's invitation, but make sure not to show how happy it makes us: we walk beside her toward the café with our lips sealed.

Though we constantly remind ourselves that others may not exist and we may be inventing them, we still suffer inexplicably from our schoolmates' disdain and from our own dull heaviness and clumsiness—we ourselves feel ashamed to be so contemptible. When others speak to us we want to hide our face in our hands, it feels so shapeless and ugly. Yet all the while we dream of someone falling in love with us: he sees us having ice cream with our mother at the café and secretly follows us home and writes us a love letter. We wait for the letter, deeply shocked each day that it hasn't yet arrived; we know its contents by heart, we've murmured them to ourselves so often. Once the letter finally arrives, we'll really have a luxuriant mystery, a secret story that will unfold totally beyond our home. For we have to admit that as of now our mystery is nothing much, there's very little hidden behind the stony face we offer our parents for their good-night kiss; after the kiss we hurriedly escape to our room while our parents whisper suspicious questions about us.

Mornings, we go to school after staring anxiously at our face in the mirror: our face has lost the velvety softness of childhood, and we regret our lost childhood, when we made mudpies and our only grief was the arguments in the house. Now they don't argue as much as they used to—our older brothers have gone off to live on their own and our parents are older and calmer. But we no longer care what goes on at home. We walk to school alone in the fog; when we were very small, our mother took us to school and came to pick us up, but now we're alone in the fog, and frighteningly responsible for everything we do.

Love thy neighbor as thyself, God said. This seems absurd. God said something absurd, commanded us to achieve the impossible. How can we love our neighbor if he rejects us and won't let himself be loved? How can we love ourselves, despicable and dull and dismal as we are? How can we love our neighbor who might not even exist, is merely a mass of shadows, while

God created us, us alone, and put us here in a world of shadows, all alone to feed on our giddy thoughts? As a child, we used to believe in God, but now we think he might not exist, or if he exists, he cares nothing about us since he put us in this cruel situation, and so it's as if he doesn't exist. Still, at dinner we refuse a dish we like, then spend the night stretched out on the rug in our room to mortify and punish ourselves for our hateful thoughts and make God love us.

But God doesn't exist, we decide after a whole night on the floor, our limbs totally stiff, shivering up and down with cold and sleepiness. God doesn't exist, because he couldn't possibly have created this absurd monstrosity of a world, this complicated scheme where a human being has to walk alone in the fog every morning amid tall buildings where her neighbor lives, the neighbor who doesn't love her and whom it is impossible to love. And one's neighbor includes that monstrous, inexplicable species, the opposite sex, endowed with the terrible capacity to bring us every sort of good or harm, endowed with that terrible secret power over us. Could this other species ever find us lovable, we who are so scorned by companions of our own sex, considered so boring and insignificant, so inept and clumsy at everything?

Then one day it happens that the most admired, the most sought after of all our classmates, the head of the class, suddenly makes friends with us. How this could have occurred, we have no idea: she suddenly cast her sky-blue gaze on us, walked us home one day, and began to appreciate us. In the afternoons she comes over to do homework: the head of the class's precious notebook is in our hands, written in her beautiful, crystal-clear handwriting in sky-blue ink; we can copy her homework, which is letter-perfect. How has such happiness befallen us? How have we managed to win this friend who's so haughty with everyone, so hard to get close to? She's ambling around our very own room, tossing her tawny ponytail right beside us, tilting her sharp profile, sprinkled with pinkish freckles, over the familiar objects in our room: it's as if some rare tropical beast, miraculously tamed, has ventured within our four walls. She walks around our room, asks where various things came from, asks to borrow a book; together we have a snack and together we spit the plum pits down onto the terrace. We who were scorned by everyone have been singled out by the most unattainable, the most unhoped-for friend. We chatter feverishly so she won't get bored in our company and abandon us forever; we let loose all our dirty words and everything we know about films and sports. Alone again, we repeat insatiably the syllables of her wonderful, sonorous name, planning a thousand things to talk about tomorrow; mad with joy, we imagine she's exactly like us in every way. The next day we try to talk to her about everything we planned, we tell her everything about us, even our giddy suspicions that people and things don't really exist. She looks askance, snickers, teases us a bit. And so we realize we've made a false move, we can't talk to her about this; we revert to sports and dirty words.

At school, meanwhile, our situation has changed dramatically: all at once everyone prizes us, seeing us highly prized by the most prized of all the girls; now our comic verses are greeted with squeals and applause; before, we couldn't even make ourselves heard in the din of voices, and now when we speak everyone stops to listen; they ask us questions, they walk arm in arm with us, they help us out in our weak subjects, in sports or with homework we can't do. The world is no longer a grotesque scheme but a simple, radiant little island peopled with friendly faces everywhere. We don't thank God for this lucky transformation of our fate because God is far from our mind; we can't think of anything except our friends' merry faces all around us, the smooth, light-hearted flow of our mornings, the funny things we said that made everyone laugh; our face in the mirror isn't dreary and shapeless, it's the face our friends are delighted to greet every morning. Sustained thus by the friendship of our own sex, we view that other species, those of the opposite sex, with less horror; we almost feel we could easily do without them, live quite happily without their approbation; we almost want to spend our whole life surrounded by our girlfriends, thinking up clever jokes to make them laugh.

Then little by little, in this crowd of friends we find one who's especially glad to spend time with us, and we realize we have countless things to say to her. She's not the head of the class, she's not greatly prized by the others, she doesn't wear flashy clothes but clothes of warm, good fabrics, like what our mother picks out for us. Walking home with her, we notice that her shoes are exactly the same as ours, simple and sturdy, not showy and flimsy like those of the other girls, and we point this out with a laugh. Gradually we discover her family's ways are just like ours: she takes frequent baths, and her mother doesn't let her go to romantic movies just as our mother doesn't. She's one of us, from the same social background. We're pretty tired, by now, of the company of the head of the class, who still comes over in the afternoon: we're fed up with repeating the same dirty words and so we act supercilious, overwhelming the head of the class with the subjects we care about—our doubts about existence; we're so supercilious and nonchalant, so arrogant that the head of the class doesn't quite get it, but gives a timid smile. We take note of the timid, cowardly smile on her lips—she's afraid of losing us. No longer spellbound by her sky-blue gaze, now when we're with the head of the class we long for the round, hazel eyes of our other friend, and the head of the class realizes this and is hurt, and we're proud of hurting her: so we too have the power to cause pain.

With our new round-eyed friend we scorn the head of the class and the other girls, so rowdy and coarse—all those dirty words they're forever repeating. Now we want to be very refined, and along with our new friend we appraise people and things from the standpoint of good and poor taste. We discover that it's in good taste to remain children as long as possible, and to our mother's great relief we get rid of all the flashy, vulgar touches we had insinuated in our dress; in our clothes as well as in our bearing and manners we aspire to a childlike simplicity. We spend marvelous afternoons with our new friend, never tiring of talking and listening. We look back with amazement on our brief friendship with the head of the class, whom we've stopped seeing: being with the head of the class was so exhausting that by the end our facial muscles were stiff with the strain of fake laughter, our eyelids burned, our skin tingled; it was exhausting to have to pretend to naughtiness, to hold back confidences and always be choosing from among our words those few that were fit to be shared with the head of the class. Being with our new friend is a great comfort. There's no pretending or holding back; our words can flow freely. We can even confide our giddy doubts about existence, and dumbfounded, she tells us she has the very same doubts. "Well, do you really exist?" we each ask, and she swears that she does, and we're thrilled beyond words.

We both regret that we're of the same sex, because if we were of different sexes we could get married and be together forever and ever. We'd never be afraid of each other, or feel ashamed or appalled. We could be quite happy now, but for this shadow on our life: not knowing whether a member of the opposite sex will ever love us. The members of the opposite sex walk alongside us, they brush past us on the street, they may even be thinking about us or have designs on us that we'll never know; they hold our destiny and our happiness in their hands. Among them might be just the right one, who could love us and whom we could love—the perfect one for us. But where is he? How to recognize him and be recognized in the city crowds? Where in the city, in which house, on which precise point on earth is the right one for us, who is like us in every way, ready to respond to all our needs, to listen to us endlessly without getting bored, to smile at our shortcomings and spend the rest of his life looking at our face? What words should we speak so that he recognizes us among thousands of others? How should we dress, where should we go to meet him?

Plagued by such thoughts, we suffer from an intense shyness in the presence of the opposite sex, for fear that the right one is among them and we might lose him by a single word. We agonize at length over every word we speak, and we speak in haste, in a choked voice: fear makes our face sullen and our movements brusque and tense; we realize this, yet we think the right person can't help but recognize us, even with our tense gestures and choked voice; if he takes no notice of us, then he's not the one: the right one will recognize us and pick us out among thousands. We wait for the right person. Waking every morning, we tell ourselves this could be the day; we dress and comb our hair with infinite care, overcoming the urge to go out in an old raincoat and shapeless shoes: he might be just around the corner. Time and again we think we're in his presence; our heart beats violently at the sound of a name, at the curve of a nose or a smile, merely because we've suddenly decided that that nose and that name and that smile belong to the person destined for us. A car with yellow tires or an old lady can make us blush violently—they might be his car and his mother: the car we'll ride in on our honeymoon, the mother who'll give us her blessing.

Then all at once we see we were mistaken, he wasn't the right one, we feel nothing at all for him, nor do we suffer over it—we have no time to suffer; the car with yellow tires, the name and the smile fade swiftly away, sinking back among the thousand superfluous things that surround our life. We have no time to suffer, we're leaving for the summer holidays and we're absolutely sure that this summer we'll meet the right person. We hardly mind parting from our round-eyed friend, sure as we are that the train is carrying us to the right person, and our friend, for her part, is sure of the same thing for herself. Who can say why we're suddenly so sure the right person will turn up on a summer holiday? The long summer months go by, tedious and lonely; we write our friend interminable letters, and to console ourselves for the meeting that never took place we carefully collect all the compliments given us by old relatives or family friends and transcribe them for our friend; she in turn writes similar letters, with compliments on her intelligence or beauty from her old relatives. In the fall we have to admit that nothing out of the ordinary has occurred. Still, we're not disappointed: it's fall, we're happy and excited to see our friend and the other girls at school, we throw ourselves joyfully into the season, the right person might be waiting around the corner.

Then gradually we begin to break off with our friend. We find her rather dull, "bourgeoise"; she has such a mania for good taste and refinement. Now we want to be poor; we're drawn to a group of poor classmates and take pride in going to their unheated houses every day. We take pride in wearing our old raincoat: we still count on meeting the right person, but he'll have to love our old raincoat, love our shapeless shoes and cheap cigarettes and bare, chapped hands. As evening draws on we walk alone in our old raincoat past the houses on the edge of the city: we've discovered the outskirts, with the signs for little bars along the river;

in a trance, we linger in front of tiny shops hung with long pink undershirts, workers' coveralls, and coffee-colored underpants; we're enchanted by a shop window displaying old postcards and old hairpins: we like everything old, dusty, and shabby, we go hunting through the city for dusty, shabby things. The rain comes down in buckets on our bare head and our old raincoat isn't waterproof; we have no umbrella, we'd rather die than carry an umbrella; we have no umbrella, no hat, no gloves, no carfare—all we have in our pocket is a dirty handkerchief, some crushed cigarettes and a few kitchen matches.

We've made up our mind that the poor are our fellow men, the neighbors we must love. We scrutinize the poor people coming and going around us, watching for the chance to help a blind beggar cross the street or offer our arm to some old woman who slipped in a puddle; timidly, with the tips of our fingers, we stroke the dirty hair of the children playing in the alleys; we go home soaked to the skin, chilled, and exultant. We're not poor, we won't be spending the night on a park bench, we're not eating murky soup out of a tin pot. We're not poor, but that's only by accident—tomorrow we could be poverty-stricken.

Meanwhile the friend we've dropped is hurt on our account, just as the head of the class was hurt when we dropped her. We know this but we have no regrets, indeed we feel a kind of covert pleasure, for if someone suffers on our account, it shows we have the power to cause pain, we who for so long felt utterly weak and insignificant. It doesn't occur to us that maybe we're being harsh and cynical, because it doesn't occur to us that our friend is our neighbor too; nor do we think our parents are our neighbors: our neighbor is the poor. Sternly, we regard our parents sitting at their brightly lit table, eating their wholesome food; we're eating the same wholesome food, but just by chance—this will last only a little while longer: soon we'll have nothing but a crust of dark bread and a tin pot.

One day we meet the right person. We don't feel anything much because we don't recognize him: we walk together through the outskirts of town, little by little we get in the habit of taking walks together every day. Now and then, absentmindedly, we wonder if we might possibly be walking with the right person, but we tend to think not. We're too calm. The earth and sky haven't changed, the minutes and hours flow calmly, no bells peal in our heart. We've already been mistaken so many times, thinking we were in the presence of the right person, but he wasn't. We were overwhelmed, in the presence of these false right people, by such violent turmoil that we hardly had strength left to think— it was like living in the midst of a burning village. Trees, houses, everything was bursting into flames all around us. Then all at once the fire was out, leaving nothing but a few tepid embers. We've left behind so many burnt-out villages, we can't even count them. Now nothing is burning. For weeks, months, we spend our days with the right person without knowing it, only sometimes when we're alone we think about him, the curve of his lips, certain gestures and inflections of his voice, and at the thought of them our heart leaps ever so slightly, but we take no notice of such a muted little leap. The strange thing is that we always feel so good, so at peace with him; we can breathe freely; our brow, for years so furrowed and sullen, suddenly relaxes; we never tire of talking and listening. We realize we've never had a relationship like this with any human being; all human beings, after a while, come to seem quite harmless, simple and small. Walking beside us at his own distinct pace, with his austere profile, this person possesses an infinite power over us: he can do us any kind of good or harm. And yet we feel a boundless tranquillity.

And we leave our home and go to live with him forever. Not that we're convinced he's the right person, in fact we're not at all convinced; we still suspect the real right person is hiding somewhere in the city, who knows where. But we have no urge to find him: we'd have very little to say to him now, since we say everything to the person we're living with, maybe not the right one; we want to accept life's good and evil from him and with him. Sometimes violent conflicts erupt between us, yet they cannot destroy that boundless inner peace. And only years later, many years later, after a dense web of habits and memories and violent conflicts has been woven between us, do we finally know that he truly was the right person and we couldn't have lived with anyone else; only in him could we seek all our heart requires.

Now, in this new home we've made for ourselves, we no longer want to be poor, we're even a little frightened of being poor. We feel a curious fondness for the things around us, for a table or a rug, we who would always spill ink on our parents' rugs; this new fondness of ours for a rug is somewhat troubling, we're somewhat ashamed of it. We still walk through the streets at the edge of the city now and then, but back home we carefully wipe our muddy shoes on the doormat. We take a new pleasure in sitting at home under the lamp, the shutters sealed against the dark city. We don't feel much need for friends anymore, because we tell all our thoughts to the person who lives with us, eating our soup together at our brightly lit table: it hardly seems worthwhile to tell anyone else anything.

We give birth to children, and our fear of poverty grows. Indeed we harbor endless fears—every possible danger or suffering that might strike our children in their mortal flesh. We never used to feel our own flesh, our own body, as so fragile and mortal. We were ready to fling ourselves into the wildest adventures, always ready to take off for the most far-flung places, among lepers and cannibals: the prospect of war or epidemics or cosmic disasters left us totally unmoved. We never knew our bodies could harbor such fear, such fragility; we never dreamed we could feel so bound to life by a bond of fear, of excruciating love. How strong and free our stride was when we walked alone through the city, as if we could go on forever! We used to pity the families strolling down the avenues on Sundays, the mothers and fathers slowly pushing the baby carriages; they looked so dull and dreary. Now we're one of those families strolling slowly down the avenues pushing the carriage, and we're not dreary, we may even be happy, but it's a happiness that's hard to acknowledge, given our panic at possibly losing it forever, from one moment to the next. The baby we're pushing in the carriage is so small and weak, the love that binds us to him so painful and terrified! We're afraid of a puff of wind, a cloud in the sky—is it going to rain? We who strode bareheaded through heavy rain, sloshing through puddles! We carry an umbrella now. We'd even like to have an umbrella stand in the front hall. We're seized by the strangest longings we could never have imagined when we wandered alone and free through the city: we'd like an umbrella stand and a coat rack, sheets, towels, a country-style oven, an icebox. We don't seek out the city limits anymore; we walk along the avenues, past houses and gardens; we're careful to keep our children away from people who look too dirty and poor, for fear of lice and disease; we flee beggars.

We love our children in such a painful, frightened way that it seems no one else was ever our neighbor, or could ever be again. We're not quite used to our children's presence in the world; we're still stunned and unhinged at their turning up in our life. We have no friends anymore, or rather, if our child gets sick, we suddenly feel a flash of hatred for those few friends we do have; it almost seems their fault, for it was in their company that we were distracted from our single, excruciating love. We don't have a vocation anymore; we used to have a vocation, a beloved craft, and now if we give it the slightest attention we immediately feel guilty and rush right back to that single, excruciating love.

A sunny day, a green landscape signify only that our child can play in the grass and get rosy cheeks in the sun: we ourselves have lost every capacity for pleasure or contemplation. We regard everything with frantic suspicion, keeping an eye out for rusty nails, cockroaches, dangers for our child. We'd like to live in clean, wholesome towns with clean animals and well-bred people; the wild alluring universe lures us no more.

How stupid we've grown, we sometimes think bitterly, studying our child's head, so familiar, more familiar than anything in the world has ever been, watching him sit and make a mudpie with his chubby hands. How stupid we've grown, and how trite and dull our thoughts are, trite enough to fit in a nutshell, and yet so exhausting, so suffocating! What has become of the wild world that once lured us, where is our strength, the free, lively rhythm of our youth with its intrepid discovery of new things each day, our proud, resolute gaze, our exultant stride? Where is our neighbor now? Where is God now? Only when our child is sick do we remember to call on God: we tell him to let all our teeth and hair fall out, but make our child well. As soon as the child is well we forget God; we still have all our teeth and hair, and we take up our dull, exhausting little thoughts all over again—rusty nails, roaches, green pastures, cream of wheat. We've grown superstitious as well. We're constantly knocking on wood; if we sit down to work, to write, we'll jump up to knock on wood and turn the light on and off three times—it suddenly seems this alone can save us from disaster. We fend off sorrow; we feel it coming and hide behind chairs, behind curtains, so it can't find us.

But sorrow does find us. We've been expecting it, but we don't recognize it right away; we don't call it by its name at first. Stunned and incredulous, trusting that everything will turn out all right, we walk down the steps of our house and close that door forever. We walk endlessly down dirt roads. We're pursued and we hide: we hide in convents and in woods, in barns and in alleys, in the holds of ships and in cellars. We learn to ask for help from whoever comes along: we don't know if he's a friend or enemy, if he'll rescue us or betray us, but we have no choice, and for that instant we entrust him with our life. We also learn to give help to whoever comes along. And we cling to the faith that very soon, in a few hours or a few days, we'll return to our house with the rugs and the lamps, we'll be caressed and comforted, our children will sit playing in clean overalls and red slippers. We sleep with our children in train stations, on church steps, in shelters for the poor: we're poor, we think with no trace of pride; every trace of our childhood pride has disappeared. We're genuinely hungry, genuinely cold. We're not afraid anymore: fear has seeped inside us to merge with our exhaustion and emerge in our withered gaze, oblivious to everything around us.

Only at moments, from the depths of our exhaustion, does a true awareness of things surge up, so piercing it brings tears to our eyes: we may be looking at the earth for the last time. Never before have we felt so potent a love linking us to the dust of the roads, to the shrill cries of the birds, to the panting rhythm of our breath. But we feel more powerful than that panting rhythm, so muffled and distant that it seems no longer our own. Never before have we loved our children so deeply, their weight in our arms, their hair brushing our cheek. We don't even fear for our children anymore: we ask God to protect them, if that is his will. Thy will be done, we tell him.

Now we are truly adult, we think one morning, staring in the mirror at our grooved, hollowed face: we stare without pride and without curiosity. Simply with compassion. We have a mirror again, and four walls; who knows, maybe soon we'll have another rug, maybe even a lamp. But we have lost the people we love most, so who cares about rugs and red slippers now? We learn to put away and take care of what belonged to the dead, to return alone to the places we used to go with them, to ask questions of the silence all around. We're no longer afraid of death, we gaze at death every hour, every minute, recalling its great silence on the face we loved the most.

Now we are truly adult, we think, stunned that this is what being adult means, nothing at all like what we thought it meant as children, certainly not self-confidence, certainly not a serene mastery over all worldly things. We are adult because we carry with us the mute presence of the dead, from whom we ask counsel in our present actions, from whom we ask forgiveness for past offenses; we'd like to rip away all our past cruelties of word and deed, from the time when we still feared death but had no idea, couldn't yet fathom, how irreparable and irremediable death was. We are adult because of all the silent answers, all the silent pardons of the dead that we carry within. We are adult by virtue of that brief moment when we looked at life head-on, when we looked at all the things of this world as if for the last time and renounced them for good, restoring them to the will of God. And suddenly all the things of this world, including human beings, appeared in their just and proper proportions under heaven, while we ourselves stood suspended, regarding it all from the single proper place accorded to us. People, things, memories, all were self-evident, all in their proper place under heaven. In that brief moment we found equilibrium in our fluctuating life, and it feels that we'll always be able to retrieve that secret moment and find in it words for our craft and words for our neighbor; we'll be able to cast a free, just gaze on our neighbor, not the timorous or scornful gaze of one who is always wondering, in the presence of his neighbor, whether he will be master or servant.

All our life, we knew only how to be master or servant, but in that secret moment, that moment of complete equilibrium, we understood that there is no true mastery or true servitude on earth. So whenever we retrieve our secret moment, we'll be seeking to discover if others have ever experienced such a moment or if they are still far from it: this is what we need to find out. It is the greatest moment of a person's life, and we need to be with others whose eyes are fixed on the greatest moment of their destiny.

We're surprised to find, as adults, that we haven't lost our ancient shyness vis-à-vis our neighbor: life has not served in the least to free us from timidity. We're still timid. Only it doesn't matter now: we've earned the right to be timid; we're timid without timidity, boldly timid. Timidly, we seek out the right words. And we rejoice to find them, timidly but almost effortlessly; we rejoice to possess all those words, so many words for our neighbor that we're practically drunk with fluency and ease. And the history of our human relations never ends, for after a time they start to become too easy, too natural and spontaneous, so spontaneous and effortless that all richness and discovery and choice are gone: they end up merely as habit and complacency, an intoxication of ease. We think we can always return to our secret moment and draw forth the right words, but that's not so, for very often our returns are false returns: our eyes light up with a false gleam, we feign concern and warmth for our neighbor while in truth we've withdrawn again, huddled and frozen in our heart of darkness. Human relations must be rediscovered and reinvented every day. We must always remember that every single encounter with our neighbor is a human action, and therefore always good or evil, truth or lie, generosity or transgression.

We are so adult now that our adolescent children are already starting to look at us with eyes of stone. We're hurt, though we know quite well what this look means; we remember well having had that identical look. We're hurt and aggrieved, we whisper suspicious questions, all the while knowing so well how the long chain of human relations takes its course, making its long and inevitable parabola, the whole long road we have to travel to feel, at last, a bit of compassion.

1953

winter in the abruzzi

*Deus nobis haec otia fecit.**

I n the Abruzzi there are just two seasons: summer and winter. Spring is snowy and windy like winter, and autumn is hot and clear like summer. Summer begins in June and ends in November. Gone are the long sun-baked days on the low, parched hills, the yellow dust of the streets and the children's dysentery; winter sets in. People stop living in the streets; barefoot children disappear from the church steps. In the village I speak of, nearly all the men would vanish after the last harvests, going off to work in Terni, in Sulmona, in Rome. It was a village of bricklayers, and a number of the houses were elegantly built, with terraces and balustrades like small villas, so when you entered it was startling to find huge dark kitchens with prosciutti hanging from the ceiling, and vast, dreary, empty rooms. The kitchen fires would be lit; there were various kinds of fires—big ones made of oak logs, fires of leaves and branches, and fires made of dry twigs picked up one by one along the road. It was easy to distinguish the poor from the rich by their fires, easier than judging by the houses and the people, or their clothing and shoes, which were more or less the same for everyone.

* "God has granted us this respite." Virgil, *Eclogues*, I, v. 6.

[35]

When I first came to the village, all the faces seemed the same to me; the women, rich and poor, young and old, all looked alike. Nearly all had missing teeth: the women down there lose their teeth at thirty, from hard work and poor nutrition as well as from the strains of childbirth and nursing babies that come one after the other relentlessly. But soon, little by little, I could single out Vincenzina da Secondina, Annunziata da Addolorata, and I started visiting all the houses and warming myself at their various fires.

As the first snows began to fall, a slow sadness took hold of us. Our lot was exile. Our city was far away, our books, our friends, the shifting ups and downs of a real existence, all far away. We would light our green stove with the long pipe running across the ceiling; we used to gather in the room with the stove— we cooked and ate there, my husband wrote at the big oval table and the children scattered their toys on the floor. A picture of an eagle was painted on the ceiling, and I would stare at the eagle, thinking that that was exile. Exile was the eagle, it was the humming green stove, it was the vast, silent countryside and the motionless snow. At five o'clock the bells of the church of Santa Maria rang and the women, with their black shawls and red faces, went to prayers. Every evening my husband and I took a walk, every evening arm in arm, our feet plunged in snow. The people on our street were all friendly and familiar, and would come to their doors to greet us: "A good evening to you." Now and then someone would ask: "Well, when are you going back home?" My husband would say, "When the war is over." "And when will this war be over? You're a professor, you know everything—when will it be over?" They called him "the professor" because they couldn't pronounce his name, and they came from far and wide to consult him on all kinds of matters—the best time of year to have their teeth pulled, municipal subsidies, every variety of taxes.

In winter some old person would die of pneumonia, the bells of Santa Maria tolled the death knell, and Domenico Orecchia, the carpenter, built the casket. A woman went crazy and was taken to the asylum at Collemaggio and the whole town talked about it for quite a while. She was young and clean, the cleanest woman in the village: they said it must have been because of her great cleanliness. Girl twins were born to Gigetto di Calcedonio, who already had boy twins, and he made a big fuss in the town hall because they wouldn't give him a subsidy, seeing as he owned several acres of land and a vegetable garden as big as seven cities. Rosa, the school caretaker, had a neighbor who spit in her eye, and she went around with a bandage on it in order to collect damages: "Eyes are sensitive and spit is salty," she explained. And they talked about this for quite some time too, until there was nothing left to say.

We grew more homesick every day. It was even pleasant at times, mildly heady, like being in the company of close friends. Letters from our city came bearing news of weddings and deaths we couldn't take part in. At times the nostalgia turned sharp and bitter, turned into hatred: then we hated Domenico Orecchia, Gigetto di Calcedonio, Annunziatina, and the bells of Santa Maria. But we kept this hatred hidden, knowing it to be unjust, and our house was always full of people, some come to ask and others to offer favors. Sometimes the little dressmaker came to make us *sagnoccole*. She would tie a dish towel around her waist and beat eggs, and send Crocetta all over town to find someone who could lend us a big enough pot. Her red face was absorbed in her work and her eyes glittered with an imperious will. She would have let the house go up in flames just to have her *sagnoccole* turn out good. Her clothes and hair grew white with flour, as the strips of dough were carefully spread out on the oval table where my husband used to write.

Crocetta was our cleaning woman. She wasn't a woman, actually, since she was only fourteen years old. The dressmaker found her for us. The dressmaker divided the world into two camps: those who comb their hair and those who don't. You have to steer clear of those who don't comb their hair, for of course they have lice. Crocetta combed her hair, and therefore she came to work for us and told the children long stories of deaths and cemeteries. Once upon a time there was a child whose mother died. His father married a new wife and this stepmother didn't love the boy. So she killed him while the father was out in the fields, and made a stew out of him. The father came home and ate, but when he finished, the bones left on the plate started singing:

> My stepmother mean and cruel
> Cooked me into a gruel
> And my greedy father ate
> Every bite upon his plate.

The father killed his wife with a scythe and hung her from a nail on the front door. Sometimes I catch myself humming the words of this song, and then the whole village rises up before me, bringing the special flavor of its seasons, the icy gusts of wind, the sound of the bells.

I took my children out every morning. People were shocked and scolded me for exposing them to the cold and snow. "What sin did these poor creatures commit?" they would say. "This is no weather for walking, Signora. Go back home." We took long walks through the deserted white countryside, while the rare people we met up with looked pityingly at the children. "What sin did they commit?" Down there if a baby is born in winter they don't take him outdoors till summertime. At noon my husband would join me with the mail, and we all went home together.

I told the children about our city. They were very small when we left, and had no memories of it. I told them how the houses had many floors and there were lots of streets and buildings and beautiful stores. "But here we have Girò's," the children said.

Girò's shop was right opposite our house. Girò stood in the doorway like an old owl, his round, impassive eyes fixed on the street. He sold a little of everything—groceries, candles, postcards, shoes, oranges. When the goods arrived and Girò unloaded the cartons, the children would run over to eat the rotten oranges he threw away. At Christmas, almond nuggets and liquors and candies arrived too. But he would never give an inch on the prices. "You're so mean, Girò," the women said. And he'd retort, "If you're good you get eaten alive." At Christmas the men returned from Terni and Sulmona and Rome, stayed a few days, then left after slaughtering the pigs. For several days people ate nothing but pork sausages and scraps of fried bacon, and did nothing but drink. Then the cries of the new piglets would fill the streets.

In February the air grew damp and soft. Heavy gray clouds drifted across the sky. One year during the thaw, the gutter pipes burst. Water poured into the houses till the rooms were virtual swamps. It was like this all over town; not a single house was dry. The women emptied buckets out the windows and swept water from the doorsteps. Some people slept under open umbrellas. Domenico Orecchia said it was a punishment for some sin. This went on for more than a week, until at last every trace of snow was gone from the rooftops and Aristide repaired the pipes.

The end of winter awakened a vague restlessness in us. Maybe someone would come to visit, maybe something would finally happen. Surely our exile, too, must have an end. The roads cutting us off from the world seemed shorter, the mail came more often. All our chilblains slowly healed.

There is a certain dull uniformity in human destiny. The course of our lives follows ancient and immutable laws, with an ancient, changeless rhythm. Dreams never come true, and the instant they are shattered, we realize how the greatest joys of our life lie beyond the realm of reality. The instant they are shattered we are sick with longing for the days when they flamed within us. Our fate spends itself in this succession of hope and nostalgia.

My husband died in Regina Coeli prison in Rome a few months after we left the village. When I confront the horror of his solitary death, of the anguished choices that preceded his death, I have to wonder if this really happened to us, we who bought oranges at Girò's and went walking in the snow. I had faith then in a simple, happy future, rich with fulfilled desires, with shared experiences and ventures. But that was the best time of my life, and only now, now that it's gone forever, do I know it.

1944

my craft

My craft is writing—this I know well and have known for a long time. I hope I won't be misunderstood: about the value of what I write, I know nothing. I know that writing is my craft. When I sit down to write, I feel supremely at ease, supremely sure of being in my own element; I use tools that are familiar and habitual and feel firm in my hands. If I do anything else, study a foreign language, say, or try to learn history or geography or stenography, if I try to speak in public or knit or travel, I'm in pain, constantly wondering how others manage those things; I always feel there must be some proper way to do them that others know and I don't. I feel deaf and blind and have a kind of deep-down nausea. But when I write I never think maybe other writers know some better way of doing it. I don't care in the least how other writers go about it. Let me be clear: I can only write stories. If I try writing a critical essay or newspaper article on request, it goes fairly badly; I have to labor to find the words somewhere outside myself. I do it a bit better than studying a foreign language or speaking in public, but only a bit. And I always have the impression of cheating the reader with words borrowed or pilfered here and there. I suffer and feel like

[41]

I'm in exile. But when I write stories I'm like someone in her native land, on streets known since childhood, among her very own walls and trees. My craft is writing stories, either invented or recalled from my own life but stories nonetheless, not grounded in learning, only in memory and imagination. This is my craft, and I will do it till my dying day. I'm very happy with this craft and wouldn't change it for anything in the world. I realized it was my craft a long time ago. Between the ages of five and ten, I wasn't yet sure; I toyed with the notion that I might paint, or maybe capture territories on horseback or invent very important new machines. But since the age of ten I've known for certain, and began struggling as best I could with novels and poetry. I still have those poems. The earliest ones are clumsy, with bungled lines, but still rather entertaining; then as time went on I gradually began writing poems that were less clumsy but more and more dull and idiotic. I didn't know this, though. I was ashamed of the clumsy poems and thought the not so clumsy but idiotic ones were very good. I always thought that some day or other a famous poet would discover them and have them published and write long articles about me; I conjured up their words and sentences, composing entire articles in my mind. I thought I would win the Fracchia Prize—I had heard this was a prize given to writers. Since I was unable to publish my poems in book form, not being acquainted with any famous poet at the time, I copied them out neatly in a notebook, drew a little flower on the title page, made a table of contents and so on. Writing poems had become easy for me. I wrote almost one a day. I found that if I didn't feel like writing, all I had to do was read some poems by Pascoli or Gozzano or Corazzini and I'd suddenly get the urge. I'd come up with Pascolian or Gozzanian or Corazzinian poems, then finally poems in the style of D'Annunzio, when I discovered him as well. Still, I never thought I would be writing poetry all my life; sooner or later I wanted to write novels. I wrote three or four during those years. One was called *Marion or the Gypsy*, and another was called *Molly and Dolly* (a comic detective story), and another was called *A Woman* (in the manner of D'Annunzio, told in the second person, the story of a woman abandoned by her husband; it also had a black cook, I remember), then there was a very long, complicated one with frightening tales of kidnapped girls and carriages—I was even afraid to write it when I was alone in the house. I don't remember anything from it except one sentence I loved; it brought tears to my eyes as I wrote it: "He said, 'Ah! Isabella is leaving.'" The chapter ended with that sentence, which was very significant since the man who spoke it was in love with Isabella but didn't realize it, hadn't yet admitted it to himself. I don't recall anything about the man; I think he might have had a reddish beard. Isabella had long black hair with blue highlights, who knows what else. I do know that for a long time I shivered with joy whenever I repeated to myself, "Ah! Isabella is leaving." I also often repeated a sentence I had found in a serialized novel in the back pages of *La Stampa* that went, "Assassin of Gilonne, what have you done with my child?" But I wasn't as confident about my novels as I was about my poems. Reading them over, I would always discover some weakness, something wrong that ruined everything and that was impossible to fix. For one thing, I constantly mixed up ancient and modern times; I couldn't place them properly in any period. There would be convents and carriages and a French Revolution atmosphere mixed in with police carrying nightsticks, then all of a sudden a proper little gray-haired lady with sewing machines and cats would turn up, as in Carola Prosperi's books, and she didn't fit well at all with the carriages and convents. I vacillated between Carola Prosperi and Victor Hugo and the Nick Carter stories, not really knowing what I wanted to do.

I also loved Annie Vivanti. There's a line in *The Devourers*, when she writes to an unknown man and tells him, "My clothes are brown." This too was a sentence I often repeated to myself. Throughout the day I'd murmur those phrases I loved so much—"Assassin of Gilonne," "Isabella is leaving," "My clothes are brown"—and I was gloriously happy.

Writing poetry was easy. I was very pleased with my poems; they seemed almost perfect. I couldn't see how they were any different from real poems, published poems by real poets. I couldn't understand why when I showed them to my brothers they snickered and said I'd be better off studying Greek. Most likely, I thought, my brothers didn't know much about poetry. Meanwhile I had to go to school and study Greek, Latin, mathematics and history, and I suffered enormously and felt I was in exile. I spent my days writing my poems and copying them into notebooks, and didn't study my lessons, then I would set the alarm for five in the morning. The alarm rang but I didn't get up. I got up at seven, when there was no time left to study and I had to get dressed for school. I was unhappy, always feeling terribly frightened and guilty and confused. At school I studied history during Latin class and Greek during history class, and I learned nothing this way. For a good while I thought it was worth it because my poems were so wonderful, but at a certain point I began to suspect maybe they weren't so wonderful; I began to feel bored writing them, struggling to find subjects; it seemed I had already plumbed every possible subject, used up every word and rhyme: *speranza lontananza, pensiero mistero, vento argento, fragranza speranza.* I had nothing left to say. That was the start of a very bleak period for me. I spent afternoons tinkering with words that no longer gave me any pleasure, full of guilt and shame about school. It never crossed my mind that I was mistaken about my craft; I wanted to write as much as ever, only I couldn't understand why all at once my days had become so barren and stripped of words.

The first serious thing I wrote was a story. A short story, five or six pages: it miraculously wrote itself in one evening, and when I went to sleep I was exhausted, dazed, and astounded. I could sense it was something serious, for the first time ever: the poetry and the novels with girls and carriages suddenly seemed very far away, naïve and absurd creatures from another age, a vanished epoch. This new story had characters. Isabella and the man with the reddish beard weren't characters; I didn't know anything about them besides the words and phrases I had used to describe them; they had been entrusted to chance and to my own willful caprice. The words and phrases I had used for them were plucked out by chance—it was as if I had a sack and had fished things out at random, a beard and a black cook and anything else that might serve. This time, though, it wasn't a game. This time I had invented people with names I couldn't possibly have changed. I couldn't have changed anything about them, and I knew a great many details about them; I knew what their life had been like up to the moment of my story, even if I didn't mention any of that in the story—it hadn't been necessary. And I knew all about the house and the bridge and the moon and the river. I was seventeen years old and had failed Latin, Greek, and mathematics. I wept when I heard the news. But once I had written the story, I felt a little less ashamed. It was summer, a summer night. The window was open onto the garden and dark butterflies were fluttering around the light. I had written my story on squared paper and I felt happier than I had ever felt in my life, rich with words and ideas. The man was called Maurizio and the woman was called Anna and the baby was called Villi, and there were also the bridge and the moon and the river. Those things lived within me. And the man and the woman weren't good or bad, only comical and slightly wretched, and I thought I had discovered just what people in books should always be—comical and wretched at once. From whatever angle I regarded it, the story was wonderful: there were no wrong moves, everything happened at the right moment, the timing was perfect. Now, I thought, I could write millions of stories.

And I actually did write quite a few, one every month or two, some fairly good and some not. I learned it was exhausting to write seriously. It's a bad sign if you're not exhausted. You cannot expect to produce something serious in any casual way, with one hand tied behind you, as it were, flitting around as the spirit moves you. You can't get off so easily. When you write something serious, you sink into it and drown right up to your eyes, and if you happen to be assailed by strong emotions, if you're very happy or very unhappy for some reason—call it terrestrial—which has nothing to do with what you're writing, then to the extent that the writing is valid and worthy of life, every other feeling will become dormant. You cannot expect to preserve your precious happiness fresh and intact, nor your precious unhappiness; everything recedes, disappears, and you're alone with the page; no happiness or unhappiness can survive that isn't intimately linked to that page; you possess nothing, you belong to no one, and if you don't feel this way, that is a sign that your page is worthless.

So for a while I wrote short stories, and this lasted about six years. Since I had discovered the existence of characters, I believed that simply *having* a character sufficed to make a story. Thus I was always on the prowl for characters. I studied people in the tram and on the street, and when I found a face that seemed right for a story, I would weave moral details and a little story around it. I was also on the prowl for details of clothing and appearance, or the interiors of houses and other places;

when I entered a new room I would strive to formulate a description of it and to find some minute detail that might fit well in a story. I kept a notebook where I wrote down various details I'd noticed, or little metaphors or incidents that I vowed to use in my stories. For example, I would write in my notebook: "He came out of the bath dragging the belt of his robe behind him like a long tail." "'The toilet in this house really stinks,' the girl told him. 'When I go in there I don't even breathe,' she added sadly." "Her curls like bunches of grapes." "Red and black blankets on the unmade bed." "A face as pale as a peeled potato." And yet I found it difficult to make use of these phrases when writing a story. The notebook became a kind of museum of phrases, all of them crystallized and embalmed, barely usable. I tried any number of times to stick the red and black blankets or the curls like bunches of grapes in some story, and I could never succeed. In the end, the notebook was of no use. And so I learned that in this craft there can be no savings. Supposing you think, "This is an excellent detail, but I don't want to waste it in the story I'm writing now, which already has lots of excellent material, so I'll save it for a later story." That detail will then crystallize inside you and never be of any use. When writing a story, you must toss in the best of everything you have seen and possess, the best of everything you've gathered throughout your life. Details can dissipate: if they're carried around for long periods without being used, they wear out. And not only details but everything—ideas, clever turns of phrase. In the era when I was writing my short stories, the era of my taste for well-chosen characters and minute details, I happened to see a cart pass by on the street carrying a mirror, a huge mirror with a gilt frame. It was reflecting the greenish evening sky, and I stopped to watch it go by, feeling an immense happiness, the sense that something important was taking place. I had been feeling very happy even before seeing the mirror, and suddenly I felt as though the very image of my happiness was passing by, the resplendent green mirror in its gilt frame. For a long time I thought of putting it in a story; for a long time recalling the cart with the mirror on top made me want to write. But I never managed to put it anywhere and at a certain point I realized it was dead inside me. And yet it had been of great importance. For at the time of writing those short stories I was always arrested by dismal, seedy people and things; the reality I sought was contemptible, without any splendor. There was a touch of malice in my taste for digging up minute details, an avid petty interest in tiny things, tiny as fleas. I was a dirtdigger, perversely bent on hunting for fleas. The mirror on the cart seemed to offer new possibilities, maybe the capacity to focus on a more glorious and radiant reality, a brighter reality that didn't call for minute descriptions and clever conceits but could be realized in one joyous, resplendent image.

In essence, I felt contempt for the characters in the short stories I was writing at that time. Since my discovery of the wonderful effects of comical, wretched characters, I had used comic touches and pathos to create beings so worthless and lacking in radiance that I myself couldn't love them. My characters always had tics or obsessions or some physical deformity or faintly grotesque vice; they'd have a broken arm in a black sling, or a stye in their eye, or else they would stutter or scratch their behinds while they spoke, or have a slight limp. I always found it necessary to distinguish them in some such way. It was a means of evading my fear that they would turn out amorphous, of eliciting their humanity, which I myself unconsciously had no faith in. For I didn't grasp back then—but at the moment of the mirror on the cart I was beginning murkily to grasp—that I wasn't dealing with characters but with puppets, quite well-drawn and resembling real people, but still puppets. The moment I conceived them I would define and label them with a grotesque detail, and there was something a trifle malicious in this, a kind of spiteful resentment I was feeling towards reality. It wasn't a resentment based on anything real, since I was a happy young girl at the time; rather, it arose as a reaction to my naïveté; it was that specific resentment used as a defense by naïve people, who always tend to think they're being taken in—the peasant newly arrived in the city who sees thieves everywhere. At first I was proud of this: it seemed a great triumph of irony over naïveté, and over the sentimental adolescent outpourings so apparent in my poetry. Irony and malice struck me as critical weapons to hold on to; I could use them to write like a man; I had a horror that my writing might reveal that I was a woman. I almost always created male characters who would be as remote and distinct from me as possible.

I had become quite adept at constructing a story, whisking away everything useless and inserting the details and dialogue at the right moment. I wrote dry, lucid stories, carried off smoothly from beginning to end, without clumsiness, without errors of tone. And then at some point I found I was fed up. The faces I saw in the street no longer yielded anything of interest. One had a stye and another had his hat on backwards and another was wearing a scarf instead of a shirt, but none of it mattered anymore. I was tired of looking at people and things and formulating descriptions of them. The world fell silent for me. I couldn't find words to describe it, I no longer had any words that could give me much pleasure. I had nothing. I tried to remember the mirror, but even that was dead inside me. I was hauling around a load of embalmed things, mute faces and words made of ashes, towns and voices and gestures that sent out no vibrations: a dead weight on my heart.

Then my children were born, and at first, when they were very small, I couldn't understand how anyone with children could manage to write. I didn't understand how I could ever detach myself from them to pursue some character in a story. I took to scorning my craft. Now and then I felt a desperate nostalgia for it, I felt exiled, but I forced myself to scorn it and belittle it in order to concentrate solely on my children. I thought this was what I had to do. I was preoccupied with cream of wheat and cream of barley and whether to take the children for a walk: was it sunny or not sunny, windy or not windy? The children seemed too important for me to risk losing myself in stupid stories, stupid embalmed characters. And yet I had a fierce nostalgia, and sometimes at night I could have wept, remembering how precious my craft had once been. I thought I would recover it some day or other, but I didn't know when; I thought I had to wait until my children had grown up and left home. What I felt for my children, at that point, was an emotion I hadn't yet learned to control. But after a while I did learn, little by little. It didn't even take all that much time. I was still making tomato sauce and cereal, but meanwhile I was thinking about what I would write. We were living in a beautiful village in the south back then. I would recall the streets and hills of my own city, and those streets and hills would merge with the streets and hills and fields of the village we were living in then, and out of their union came a fresh landscape that I could love anew. I was homesick for my city and loved it dearly in memory, loved it and understood its nature perhaps even better than when I had lived there, and I also loved the town we were living in, dusty and white under the southern sun, its broad fields of parched stubble spread out under my windows, while the memory of my city's boulevards with their plane trees and tall buildings sent gusts through my heart; and all of this sparked a joyous flame inside

me and I had a fierce longing to write. I wrote a long story, the
longest I had ever written. I took up writing again like someone
who had never written before: it was so long since I had written
anything that the words felt rinsed and fresh; once again everything seemed untouched, rich with flavor and scent. I wrote in
the afternoons while the children were out walking with a girl
from the village; I wrote avidly, with joy, and it was a gorgeous
autumn and I felt so happy every day. In the story, I put some
made-up people along with some real people from the village; I
even came up with a few words that were always used there and
that I hadn't known before, certain curses and local expressions,
and those new words, like yeast, fermented and made all the old
words around them rise with fresh life. The principal character
was a woman, but totally different from me. I didn't long to write
like a man anymore, for I had had children and knew all sorts of
things about tomato sauce, and even if I didn't put them in the
story, simply knowing them was useful to my craft; in some ar-
cane, mysterious way, this too served my craft. I felt that women
knew things about their children that a man could never know.
I wrote my story in great haste, as if in fear that it might escape
me. I called it a novel, but maybe it wasn't a novel. In any case, I
had always written briefly and in haste, and at some point I even
thought I understood why. It was because I had much older
brothers, and when I was small, if I spoke at the table they always
told me to be quiet. So I got used to speaking my piece quickly,
at top speed, with the fewest possible number of words, forever
afraid the others would resume their own conversations and
stop listening to me. This explanation may seem somewhat silly,
and yet that's exactly what must have happened.

As I said, that period when I was writing what I called a novel
was a very happy time for me. Nothing momentous had ever
taken place in my life, I had no knowledge of sickness and be-

trayal and loneliness and death. Nothing in my life had ever been wrecked, except for trivial things; nothing dear to my heart had ever been ripped away. I had suffered only the idle melancholies of adolescence and the pain of not knowing how to write. I was happy, back then, in a full, tranquil way, without fear or anxiety, with utter faith in the solidity and reliability of happiness in this world. When we are happy, we feel colder, clearer, more aloof from reality. When we are happy, we tend to create characters very different from ourselves, to see them in the chilly light of alienness; we shift our gaze from our satisfied, happy soul to cast judgment, quite without charity, on others—a judgment that is nonchalant and pitiless, ironic and arrogant—and all the while our imagination and creative energy are working away with vigor. We can create characters with ease, lots of characters, fundamentally unlike ourselves, and we can create solidly constructed stories that seem to have been set out to dry in a clear, cold light. What is missing, though, when we are happy in this particular way—tearless, fearless, carefree—what is missing is an intimate, loving connection with our characters, with the places and events we are writing about. What is missing is charity. To all appearances we are much more generous, in the sense that we can always find the energy to be interested in others, even to lavish our concern on them: we're not so involved with ourselves, there being no need. But that kind of interest in others, so lacking in warmth, grasps only a few very superficial aspects of their beings. We see the world in a single dimension, it holds no secrets and shadows; we do manage, thanks to the imaginative energy driving us, to intuit and create the grief we know nothing about, but we see it purely in the sterile, chilly light of things that are not truly our own, that have no roots inside us.

Our individual happiness or unhappiness, our *terrestrial* condition, has great importance for what we write. I said earlier that in the act of writing one is miraculously impelled to set aside the actual circumstances of his own life. That is certainly true. Yet being happy or unhappy leads us to write in one way or another. When we are happy our imagination is stronger; when we are unhappy, memory acts with greater force. Suffering makes the imagination feeble and lazy; it stirs, but listlessly, languidly, with the frail movements of the sick, the exhaustion and cautiousness of achy, feverish limbs; we find it difficult to shift our focus from our own life, our own spirit, the cravings and restlessness that pervade us. In our writing, memories of the past continually rise to the surface; our own voice continually reverberates, and we are powerless to silence it. A special relationship, fond and maternal, springs up between us and the characters we invent— which our languishing imagination still manages to invent—a warm relationship suffused with tears, a stifling, carnal intimacy. We have deep, doleful roots in every being and every thing in the world, a world grown full of echoes and tremors and shadows, to which we are bound by a reverent, impassioned mercy. The risk, then, is of being shipwrecked in a dark lake of still, stagnant waters and dragging our imagined characters down with us, letting them perish with us in the tepid, dark abyss, among dead rats and rotted flowers. As far as our writing is concerned, there is danger in sorrow just as there is danger in happiness. For poetic beauty is a composite of ruthlessness, arrogance, irony, carnal love, imagination and memory, of light and dark, and if we cannot achieve all of these together, our result will be impoverished, precarious, and scarcely alive.

Also bear in mind, you cannot expect your writing to console you in your sorrow. You cannot be deluded into thinking your craft will soothe or lull you. There have been interminably desolate, lonely Sundays in my life, when I longed ardently to write something to ease my loneliness and ennui, to be comforted and beguiled by words and sentences. But I couldn't manage to write a single line. At times like that my craft always turned me away, it didn't want anything to do with me. Because this craft is never a consolation or a diversion. It is no companion. This craft is a master, a master capable of drawing blood, a master who shouts and passes judgment. We have to swallow our spit and tears and grit our teeth and wipe the blood from our wounds and serve him. Serve him on demand. Only then will he help us get back up and plant our feet firmly on the ground, help us overcome madness and delirium, fever and despair. But he is always the one in charge; he turns a deaf ear to our neediness.

I came to know sorrow well after my time in the south, genuine sorrow, irreparable and incurable, that fractured my whole life, and when I tried to put it back together somehow, I found that I and my life had changed beyond recognition from what we were before. My craft remained unchanged—and yet it is profoundly deceptive to say it was unchanged: the tools were the same but the way I handled them was different. At first I detested it, it repelled me, but I knew very well that in the end I would go back to serving it and it would save me. And so it's often struck me that I haven't been quite so unfortunate in my life, and that I'm unjust to rail against destiny for showing me no benevolence, since it has given me three children and my craft. I couldn't even begin to imagine my life without my craft. It has always been there, it has never deserted me for a moment; even when I thought it lay dormant, its vigilant, radiant eye was watching over me.

Such is my craft. It doesn't yield much money, as you can see, in fact to earn a living you always need other work at the same time. Still, once in a while it does yield some small sum, and earning money from it feels so sweet, like receiving money and gifts from the hands of the one you love. Such is my craft. As I said, I can't rightly judge the merits of its results so far or to come, or rather, I can judge the relative merits of the results achieved so far, but definitely not the absolute. When I'm writing something, I usually think it is very important and that I'm a very great writer. I imagine this happens to everyone. But in the back of my mind I always know very well what I am, namely a small, small writer. I swear I know. But it doesn't much matter. Except I'd rather not name names; I have found that if I ask myself A small writer like who? it depresses me to name other small writers. I prefer to think no one has ever been quite like me, however small, however flea-like or mosquito-like a writer I may be. What does matter is having the conviction that it truly is a craft, a profession, something to follow for the rest of one's life. But as a craft, it is no joke. It has countless dangers beyond the ones I've mentioned. We are continually menaced by grave dangers in the very act of confronting the page. There is the danger of suddenly starting to tease or perform an aria. I always have a mad longing to start performing, and have to be very careful not to do so. And there is the danger of cheating with words that don't really come from within, that we have fished up from outside at random and skillfully pieced together, for we do become somewhat cunning. There is a danger in becoming cunning, in cheating. It is a very difficult craft, as you can see, but the most wonderful in the world. The daily ups and downs of our life, the daily ups and downs we witness in others' lives, all that we read and see and think and discuss feeds its hunger, and it grows within us. It is a craft that thrives on terrible things too; it feeds on the best and the worst in our life, our evil feelings and our good feelings course through its blood. It feeds on us, and it thrives.

1949

the son of man

There was the war, with so many houses collapsing all around us, and now people no longer feel safe and secure in their own houses, as once we did. Some things are incurable, and though years go by, we never recover. Even if we have lamps on the tables again, vases of flowers and portraits of our loved ones, we have no more faith in such things, not since we had to abandon them in haste or hunt for them in vain amid the rubble.

It is useless to think we can recover from twenty years of what we went through. Those of us who were persecuted will never again rest easy. For us the insistent blare of a doorbell in the middle of the night can mean only the one word, "police." And there's no use telling ourselves over and over that nowadays the word "police" may mean friendly faces we can call on for protection and help. For us this word will always trigger suspicion and fright. I can watch my sleeping children and think with relief that I won't have to wake them in the middle of the night and run away. But it is not a deep or utter relief. I always have the feeling that someday we'll have to jump up at night and run away again, leaving everything behind, quiet rooms and letters and clothing and mementos.

The experience of evil, once suffered, is never forgotten. Anyone who has seen houses collapse knows all too well how fragile vases of flowers, paintings and white walls really are. He knows all too well what a house is made of. A house is made of bricks and mortar and it can crumble. A house is nothing very solid. It can crumble from one moment to the next. Behind the serene vases of flowers, behind the teapots, the rugs and the waxed floors, is the other, the true face of the house, the horrible face of the crumbled house.

We will never be cured of this war. It is useless. We are people who will never feel at ease, never think and plan and order our lives in peace. Look what has been done to our houses. Look what has been done to us. We can never rest easy again.

We have known reality in its most somber guise and are no longer repelled by it. Some still complain that the writers use bitter, violent language and tell of hard, sad things, that they present reality in its most desolate terms.

We cannot lie in books and we cannot lie in anything else we do. This may be the one good that has come out of the war: not lying and not tolerating the lies of others. This is who we young people are now, this is our generation. Our elders are still under the spell of lies, of the veils and masks shrouding reality. Our language saddens and offends them. They cannot understand the way we see reality: we are right up against the essence of things. This is the one benefit the war has brought, but only to the young. To those who are older it has brought nothing but insecurity and fear. We young people are afraid too, we too feel unsafe in our houses, but we are not defenseless against our fear. We have a toughness and a strength that those who came before us have never known.

For some the war began simply with the war, with the crumbling houses and the Germans, but for others it started earlier, in the first years of Fascism, so that their sense of insecurity and perpetual danger is all the greater. For many of us it began long years ago—the sense of danger, of needing to hide, of suddenly having to leave the warmth of bed and home. It crept into our childhood games, it followed us to our desks at school, it taught us to see enemies everywhere. It was like that for many of us in Italy and elsewhere; we trusted that one day we would be able to walk the streets of our city in peace, but now that we can, perhaps, walk in peace, we realize we haven't gotten over the damage we suffered. And so we are constantly forced to seek new strength and new toughness to confront whatever reality might bring. We are compelled to seek an inner peace that rugs and vases of flowers cannot yield.

There is no peace for the son of man. Foxes and wolves have their dens, but the son of man has nowhere to lay his head. We are a generation of human beings, not a generation of foxes and wolves. We all long to lay our heads down somewhere, we long for a warm, dry little den. But there is no peace for the sons of men. All of us, at some point in our lives, were deluded into thinking we could lull ourselves to sleep somewhere or other, could seize upon some certainty, some faith, and finally rest our bones. But all the old certainties have been wrenched from us, and faith, in the end, has never been a place to take one's ease.

And we have no more tears. What moved our parents has no power to move us. Our parents and the older generations reproach us for the way we raise our children. They would like us to lie to our children the way they lied to us. They would like our children to play with plush dolls in pretty pink rooms with little trees and rabbits painted on the walls. They would like us to swaddle their childhood in veils and lies and keep reality in its true essence carefully hidden from them. But we cannot do it. We cannot do it with children we woke in the dead of night and dressed frantically in the dark, either to run or hide, or because the sirens were lacerating the skies. We cannot do it with children who have seen fear and horror on our faces. We cannot make ourselves tell these children that we found them under cabbages or that someone who has died has gone on a long trip.

There is a bottomless abyss between us and earlier generations. Their dangers were trivial and their houses rarely collapsed. Earthquakes and fires were not common or frequent occurrences. The women knitted and told the cook to get dinner ready and received their friends in houses that didn't collapse. They pondered and planned and expected to order their lives in peace. It was another era and maybe they were fortunate. But we are bound to this our anguish and glad, at heart, of our destiny as human beings.

1946

portrait of a friend*

The city that was dear to our friend is the same as ever. There's been some change, but nothing much: they've added trolleys, built some subways. There are no new movie houses. The old ones still remain with their long-ago names, names whose syllables, when repeated, reawaken our childhood and youth. We live elsewhere now, in a larger and altogether different city, and if we meet and talk about our city, it is with no regret at having left; we say we couldn't possibly live there now. But when we return, no sooner do we cross the entrance hall of the railway station and stroll through the mist of the avenues, than we feel right at home. And the sadness the city inspires each time we return is precisely in this feeling at home and feeling at the same time that we no longer have any reason to be there. For here at home in our own city, the city where we spent our youth, few things are still alive for us—we're greeted by a cluster of memories and shadows.

Our city, in any case, is melancholy by nature. On winter mornings it has its own special smell of station and soot, diffused

---

* Cesare Pavese

through all the streets and avenues. Arriving in the morning, we find it gray with fog, wrapped in its smell. Sometimes a faint sun filters through the fog, tingeing the heaps of snow and the bare branches of shrubbery with rose and lilac. The snow on the streets and boulevards has been shoveled and gathered in little piles, but the public gardens are still buried under a thick blanket, soft and intact, an inch high on the abandoned benches and the rims of the fountains; the clock on the riding path has stopped, from time immemorial, at a quarter to eleven. Across the river rises the hill, it, too, white with snow, but dappled here and there with a reddish stubble, and at the top towers a round, rust-colored building that was once the National Balilla Organization.* With a bit of sunlight, the glass cupola of the Auto Exhibition Hall glistens and the river flows with a greenish sparkle under the great stone bridges, and then for an instant the city can seem bright and welcoming, but this is a fleeting impression. The city's essential nature is melancholy: the river, vanishing in the distance, evaporates in a horizon of violet mists that suggest sunset even if it's high noon, and everywhere you breathe the same somber, drudging smell of soot and hear the whistle of trains.

Our city, we realize now, resembles the friend we lost, who loved it dearly. It is industrious, as he was, frowning in its fevered, stubborn busyness, yet at the same time indolent, inclined to be idle and dream. In this city that so resembles him, we sense our friend come to life again wherever we go. At every corner, at every turn it seems he might suddenly appear—the tall figure in his dark martingale coat, face hidden in the collar, hat pulled down over his eyes. Stubborn and solitary, our friend paced the city with his long stride. He used to hide out in the most secluded and smoky cafes, where he would hurriedly throw

---

* Fascist Youth Organization

off his overcoat and hat, but keep his ugly little light-colored scarf flung around his neck; he would twist long strands of his brown hair around his fingers, then suddenly muss up his hair with a lightning gesture. He filled pages and pages with his broad, swift writing, crossing out furiously, and in his poetry he commemorated the city:

> This is the day the mists rise from the river
> In the beautiful city, amidst the meadows and hills,
> Sending it up in smoke like a memory....

His poems echo in our ears whenever we return to the city or think of it, and we can't even tell anymore if they are beautiful poems—they are so much a part of us, they reflect so keenly the image of our youth, those faraway days when we listened to our friend read them aloud for the first time and learned, to our profound amazement, that even from our gray, heavy, and un-poetic city, one could make poetry.

Our friend lived in the city like an adolescent, and lived that way until the end. His days, like those of adolescents, were very long, with plenty of time: he could find space to study and to write, to earn a living and to idle along the streets he loved, while we floundered, embattled, between laziness and dili-gence, wasting hours trying to figure out whether we were lazy or diligent. For many years he refused to submit to office hours or accept a regular position, but when he did agree to sit at a desk he became a scrupulous and tireless worker, all the while pre-serving an ample margin of spare time for himself: he downed his meals at top speed, eating very little, and he never slept.

He had spells of great sadness, but for a long time we thought he would get over the sadness once he made up his mind to grow up: his sadness seemed like a boy's, the voluptuous, dreamy melancholy of a boy who hasn't yet come down to earth and moves in an arid, solitary fantasy world. Sometimes he would come over to see us in the evenings; he would sit himself down, pale, the scarf around his neck, and twist his hair or crumple a sheet of paper, without uttering a single word all evening, not even answering any of our questions. At last he would abruptly seize his coat and leave. Feeling mortified, we wondered if we had disappointed him, if he had sought to cheer himself up in our company and failed, or whether he had simply decided to spend a silent evening under some lamp other than his own.

To converse with him was never easy anyway, even when he was in good spirits. And yet an encounter with him, no matter how few words were exchanged, could be stimulating and invigorating like nothing else. In his presence we became far more intelligent; we felt impelled to express whatever was best and most serious in us; we cast aside platitudes, imprecision, incoherence.

We often felt humbled in his presence, for we could not be as sober as he was, nor as unassuming, nor as generous and fair-minded. He treated us, his friends, brusquely and didn't excuse any of our faults, but if we were sick or in pain, he immediately became as solicitous as a mother. He refused on principle to meet new people, yet he could suddenly, out of the blue, become warm and expansive with someone quite unknown and unexpected, someone maybe even vaguely contemptible, lavishing his time and his plans. If we pointed out that that person was in many ways unpleasant or despicable, he said he was well aware of it, for he always liked to know everything and would never give us the satisfaction of telling him anything new. But why he would become so close with some such person and then deny his friendship to others more deserving, he would never explain and we never discovered. At times he would become intrigued by someone he thought came from an elegant milieu, and would become friendly with that person; perhaps he was gathering material for his novels. But his judgment of elegance of manner or appearance was unreliable—he took the glitter for the gold. In this and only this, he was very naïve. He was mistaken about elegance of manner, but about elegance of spirit and cultivation he could never be deceived.

He had a cautious, miserly way of shaking hands, a few fingers granted and withdrawn; he had a diffident, parsimonious way of taking tobacco out of his pouch and filling his pipe; and he had a brusque, abrupt way of giving us money if he found out we needed it, so brusque and abrupt that we were dumbfounded. He said he was stingy with money and that it hurt to part with it, but the minute he had parted with it, he didn't give a damn anymore. If we were far away he neither wrote to us nor answered our letters, or else would answer with a few curt, chilling sentences. He was unable to love his friends when they were far away, he said; he didn't want to suffer from their absence, and so he promptly reduced them to ashes in his mind.

He never had a wife or children or a home of his own. He lived with a married sister who loved him and whom he loved, yet he kept his usual brusque ways in the family, behaving like a boy, or like a stranger. At times he would come to our houses and, with a good-natured frown, scrutinize the children we were raising, the families we were making for ourselves. He too thought of having a family, but he thought of it in a way that over the years grew ever more complicated and tortuous, so tortuous that no simple resolution could possibly spring from it. Over the years he had created a network of such tangled, inexorable thoughts and principles that it barred the fulfillment of the most simple reality; and the more forbidden and unattainable that reality, the more profound was his desire to overcome it, twisting and branching out like a snaking, choking vine. He could be so sad at times, and we wanted so much to help him, but he never allowed us a sympathetic word or a comforting glance. And so it came about that we too, following his example, refused his sympathy in the hour of our own grief. Not that he was a teacher to us, although he taught us many things. We saw quite clearly the absurd and twisted mental convolutions in which he imprisoned his simple soul, and we would have liked to teach him something ourselves—how to live in some more fundamental way, with room to breathe. But we never managed to teach him anything, for whenever we tried to explain our reasoning he raised his hand and said he already knew all about it.

In his final years his face was deeply lined and hollowed, devastated by mental torments, but to the last his body kept the grace of an adolescent. Toward the end he became a famous writer, but this didn't change his retiring habits in the least, neither the modesty of his disposition nor the careful, painstaking humility he brought to his daily work. When we asked him if he enjoyed being famous he would reply, with an arrogant smirk, that he had always expected it—this cunning, arrogant smirk, childishly malevolent, would flash across his face once in a while, then disappear. But his having always expected it meant that the achievement no longer gave him any joy, for he was incapable of enjoying and loving things once he had them. He used to say he knew his art so thoroughly by now that it held no more secrets for him, and without secrets, could no longer interest him. Even we, his friends, he said, held no more secrets and bored him infinitely. We were so mortified at boring him that we couldn't tell him we saw exactly where he went wrong: in his unwillingness to give in and love the daily course of life, which proceeds uniformly and apparently without secrets. And so he was always in struggle against daily reality, both thirsting for it and loathing it; yet it was invincible and forbidden to him. He could only gaze at it as if from an infinite distance.

He died in summer. Our city is deserted in the summer and feels vast, open and resonant, like a piazza. The sky is clear but not luminous, with a milky pallor; the river runs flat as a road, giving off neither moisture nor coolness. Billows of dust rise from the avenues; huge trucks drive by, loaded with sand from the river; the asphalt of the streets is layered with pebbles baking in the tar. Out in the open, the café tables under their fringed umbrellas are scorched and deserted.

None of us were there. To die, he chose an ordinary day in that torrid August; he chose a hotel room near the railway station, wishing to die like a stranger in his very own city. He had envisioned his death in an old poem of many years ago:

> There'll be no need to leave the bed.
> Only dawn will enter the empty room.
> The window alone will clothe each thing
> in a tranquil radiance, almost a light, casting
> a gaunt shadow on the upturned face.
> The memories will be clotted shadows
> spread flat as old embers in the hearth.
> Memory will be the flame
> that yesterday still stung the burnt-out eyes.

A short time after his death we went out to the hills. Along the road were cafés with arbors of reddening grapes, games of bowls, stacks of bicycles; there were farmhouses with clusters of corncobs and cut grass spread out in stacks to dry. It was the landscape he loved—the edge of the city, the verge of autumn. We watched the September night rise on the grassy slopes and the plowed fields. We were all close friends who had known each other many years, people who had always worked and thought together. As happens with those who love each other and are grief-stricken, we tried to love each other more, to protect and take care of each other, because we felt that he, in his mysterious way, had always protected and taken care of us. More than ever, he was present on that sloping hillside.

> Every returning glance keeps a taste
> of grass, of things infused with evening sun
> on the beach. It keeps a breath of sea.
> This vague shadow is like a nocturnal sea,
> its ancient dreads and shivers skimmed by sky
> returning every evening. Dead voices
> resound like the breaking of that sea.

1957

mai devi domandarmi (*You Must Never Ask Me*) was published by Garzanti in 1970 and contains essays written over the previous seven years. Some hark back to earlier days, for example, "My Psychoanalysis" and "Laziness," whose context is the bleakness of postwar Rome. Given Ginzburg's situation at the time—the death of her husband, her aimless, bedazed state and uncertain future—their dry wit is all the more potent.

Other essays are critical or occasional pieces, represented here by "The Great Lady" and "Film," and first appeared in the *La Stampa*, newspaper where Ginzburg wrote a regular column for some years. (Though Ginzburg's speculations on Ivy Compton-Burnett's circumstances in old age, in "The Great Lady," reflect the truth and coherence of a novelist's imagination, they are rather wide of the mark in actuality. According to her biographer, Hilary Spurling, Compton-Burnett had many friends, indeed was so sought after that her housekeeper had to "keep callers at bay." Moreover, she could "radiate an energy, amusement, humor and sympathy that captivated strangers." And yet Ginzberg astutely surmises that "the great lady" saved her true and tragic voice for her work.)

This collection also shows the author scrutinizing herself under new aspects: as a reluctant tourist, in "Clueless Travelers," as a househunter, in "A Place to Live," and as a grandmother, in "The Baby Who Saw Bears." Certainly these very funny pieces strike a lighter note than usual, yet in the end they, too, are carried off by the same undertow of restless bewilderment, and by a whiff of tragic destiny.

laziness

In October of 1944 I came to Rome to find work. My husband
had died the previous winter. In Rome there was a publishing
house where he had worked for years. The publisher was away
in Switzerland at the time, but the firm had resumed business
right after the liberation of Rome, and I thought that if I asked,
they would give me a job. The prospect of asking was oppressive,
however, because I thought they would be hiring me out of pity,
since I was a widow with children to support. I would have liked
someone to give me a job without knowing me, on the basis of
my skills. The trouble was that I had no skills.

I had brooded over all this during the months of the German
occupation, which I spent in the country, in Tuscany, with my
children. The war had passed through there, followed by the
usual silent aftermath, until finally, in the quiet countryside with
its ravaged villages, the Americans arrived. We moved to Florence,
where I left the children with my parents and went on to Rome.

I wanted to work because I had no money. True, had I remained with my parents I could have managed. But the idea of
being supported by my parents was also very oppressive, and
besides, I wanted to make a home for myself and my children
again. We hadn't had a place of our own for a long time. During
those last months of the war we had lived with relatives and

friends, or in convents and inns. Driving to Rome in a car that stalled every half-hour, I dallied with fantasies of adventurous jobs, such as being a governess or covering crime for a newspaper. The major obstacle to my career plans was the fact that I didn't know how to do anything. I had never taken a degree, having dropped out when I failed Latin (a subject no one ever failed back then). I didn't know any languages except a little French, and I didn't know how to type. Aside from caring for my children, doing housework very slowly and ineptly, and writing novels, I had never done a thing in my life. Moreover, I was very lazy. My laziness didn't run to sleeping late in the morning—I've always awakened at dawn, so that getting up was no problem— but to losing an infinite amount of time idling and daydreaming. As a result I had never been able to complete any studies or projects. Applying for work at the publishing house, where they would take me on out of pity and understanding, suddenly seemed the most logical, practical idea, even though I might find their motives painful. Just around that time I had read a wonderful book called *Jeunesse sans Dieu*, by Odon de Norvath, an author I knew nothing about except that he died young, hit by a falling tree while leaving a movie house in Paris. I thought that as soon as I began work at the publishers I would translate this book I loved so much, and have them bring it out.

In Rome I took a room in a pensione near the church of Santa Maria Maggiore. The pensione's particular virtue was that it cost next to nothing. I knew from experience that during the war and right after, such pensiones tended to turn into something like barracks or encampments. This one was a cross between a pensione and a boarding school. It housed students, refugees, homeless old people. Every now and then a gong with a deep hollow ring would resound up and down the stairs, summoning people to the telephone. In the dining room, frugal communal meals were taken—

Roman cheese, boiled chestnuts, broccoli. In the course of these meals, a little bell would ring from time to time and the manager of the pensione would read aloud some of her thoughts, which were exhortations to simplicity.

I spoke to a friend who was running the firm in the publisher's absence. This friend was short and fat, as round and bouncy as a ball. When he smiled, thousands of tiny wrinkles rippled across his pale, clever, sweet Chinese-baby face. Besides running the publishing firm, he was involved in countless other activities. He said he would take me on part-time, by the hour, and when the publisher returned my position would be defined more clearly. He told me to come to the office the next morning, and also said that in my very pensione lived a girl who worked in the firm, in an administrative position: I could walk to work with her in the morning.

Back at the pensione, I climbed upstairs to knock at the door of a room two floors above mine. A pretty girl with curly brown hair and red cheeks appeared and I asked if we might walk to work together the next day. She said she had to go to some bank or other and so would be taking another route. She was polite enough, but cool and reserved. I went back down feeling vaguely despondent, overcome by a fatal sense of inadequacy. That girl must have been working for years, maybe forever; her work was administrative and therefore well-defined, necessary, and indestructible. In addition, she had a nine-year-old brother with her, whom she was supporting, while I wasn't sure if I would be able to support my own children.

I was restless all night, full of agonizing thoughts. I was convinced that the moment I entered the office everyone would discover the vast sea of ignorance and laziness inside me. I thought of the friend who had hired me, and of the publisher, far off but perhaps on his way back. I had tried to explain to my friend that

I had no degree of any kind, I didn't know English, and couldn't do anything. He had replied that it didn't matter, I would find something to do. But I hadn't told him about my laziness, my vice of slipping into a state of inertia and dreaminess as soon as I was faced with a specific task. I had never before been truly horrified by this vice, but that night I confronted it with fright and profound horror. I had always been a poor student. Everything I had ever begun just remained hanging. Villon's famous lines echoed in my ears: "Hé Dieu! si j'eusse étudié/au temps de ma jeunesse folle,/et à bonnes moeurs dédié/j'eusse maison et couche molle/mais quoi! je fuyais l'école/comme fait le mauvais enfant..."*

Actually my French wasn't even very good. Nor had my youth been especially "folle," only idle and confused.

In the morning I arrived at what would be my office: the ground floor of a small house surrounded by a garden. There was my friend, along with the girl with the red cheeks, seated in front of a calculator, and two typists. My friend had me sit at a table and handed me a sheet of paper that said, "typographic rules." And thus I learned that *perché* and *affinché* had acute accents, but *tè* and *caffè lacchè* had grave accents. He then gave me a manuscript, a translation of *Gösta Berling*. I was to proofread it and put in the accent marks. As he bounced around the room like a ball, he informed me that I needn't worry about not having a degree—our mutual boss could hardly scorn me on that account since he didn't have one himself. I asked what my next assignment would be, after *Gösta Berling*, and was appalled to realize that he hadn't any idea.

---

* "Ah, God! If only I had studied in the days of my mad youth, and learned good habits, now I'd have a house and soft bed, but look! I fled from school like a bad boy..."

I had such dread of falling into laziness that I threw myself into the revision and finished in three days. My friend proceeded to give me a copy of Lenin's wife's memoirs, in French. I hurriedly translated about thirty pages, at which point he said he had changed his mind, they wouldn't be doing that book after all. He gave me a translation of *Homo Ludens.*

One day, just at the entrance to the office, I found myself face to face with the publisher. Though I had known him for quite a while, we had barely exchanged more than two words. Now so much had happened since we had last been face to face that it was like meeting him for the first time. I felt as if he were at once a friend and a total stranger. And mingled with those feelings was the thought that he was now my boss, that is, someone who could turn me out of the office at any moment. He embraced me and blushed, because he was shy; he seemed pleased and not too amazed to find me working there, and said he looked forward to hearing my ideas and suggestions. Choked with emotion and timidity, I said perhaps they might translate and bring out *Jeunesse sans Dieu.* He didn't know the book, so I hastily told him the story of the movie house and the falling tree. He was very busy and dashed off. I didn't see him again over the next few days, but the girl with the red cheeks came to tell me that I had been hired full-time. She and I never spoke, but when we met in the corridor we smiled, linked by common memories and expectations of ringing bells and broccoli.

One day I learned that we were moving to new offices. That was too bad, for I had grown fond of the office, especially of the mandarin orange tree outside my window. The new office was downtown and had huge rooms with rugs and armchairs. I chose a small room at the end of the hall, where I could be alone and could learn to work, for I was still obsessed by feelings of inadequacy. My friend also took refuge in a room of his own. Gradually the larger rooms filled up with new typists and other staff, who would pace feverishly back and forth across the rugs, dictating endless pages to the typists. I would overhear snatches in passing, but understood none of it. Or they would hold lengthy, mysterious meetings with visitors in the conference room. My friend said that he found all these new employees and new typists quite pointless. He found the rugs, the visitors and the meetings pointless as well. I grasped that the new people's politics were different from his own. He seemed depressed and didn't bounce anymore, but sat apart and inert at his desk, his face no longer crinkling up in smiles but sad and wan, like the moon. And seeing him grown so discouraged and limp, it suddenly struck me that he might be just like me and maybe even more so—sick with a boundless passivity.

I felt very alone in that office. I never said a word to anyone, and I worried constantly about being found out: my vast ignorance and laziness, my absolute dearth of ideas. By the time I got around to asking about the rights to *Jeunesse sans Dieu*, I found they had already been bought by another firm. That was my only idea and it vanished into thin air. To guard against my laziness I worked furiously, dizzily, immersed in total isolation and utter silence. Yet I couldn't help but wonder, all the while, how and if my work was connected to the intense and, to me, incomprehensible life swarming and filling the other rooms. I had a key made and went to the office even on Sundays.

January, 1969

my psychoanalysis

I once resorted to psychoanalysis. It was the summer just after the war, a sweltering, dusty summer, and I was living in Rome. My analyst's apartment was downtown. I saw him every day at three o'clock. He would let me in himself (he had a wife, but I never saw her). His office was dim and cool. Dr. B. was a tall, elderly man with a little crown of silver curls, a small gray mustache, and narrow, slightly hunched shoulders. His shirts, always immaculate, were unbuttoned at the collar. He had an ironic smile and a German accent. He wore a large brass ring with engraved initials, and his hands were white and delicate, his eyes ironic, his glasses rimmed with gold. He had me sit at a table and he sat opposite me. There was always a tall glass of water for me on the table, with an ice cube and a twist of lemon. At that time nobody in Rome had a refrigerator; if you wanted ice you had to order it from the local dairy and pound it to pieces with a hammer. How he managed to procure those smooth, clear ice cubes every day has remained a mystery. Maybe I should have asked him, but I never did. I felt that beyond the office and the little hall leading to it, the rest of the house was, of necessity, shrouded in mystery. The water and ice came from the kitchen, where perhaps the invisible wife had prepared it for me.

The friend who had recommended Dr. B., and who was also seeing him herself, hadn't told me much about him. She said he was Jewish, German, and a Jungian. The fact that he was a Jungian seemed a good sign to her, but to me was immaterial since I had confused notions about the difference between Jung and Freud. In fact one day I asked Dr. B. to explain this difference to me. He spun out an elaborate explanation and at some point I lost the thread and got distracted gazing at his brass ring, the little silver curls over his ears, and his wrinkled brow, which he wiped with a white linen handkerchief. I felt like I was in school, where I used to ask for explanations and then get lost thinking of other things.

This feeling of being in school and in the presence of a teacher was one of my many errors in the course of the analysis. Dr. B. had told me I should write my dreams in a notebook, and so before going to see him I would sit down in a café and hurriedly scribble out my dreams, with the breathless anxiety of a student who has to hand in homework. I should have felt like a sick person with a doctor, but I didn't feel sick, only full of obscure guilt and confusion. And he didn't seem to be a real doctor, either. I would sometimes study him through the eyes of my parents, who were far away up north, and I imagined that they wouldn't have liked him at all. He was nothing like the sort of people they associated with. They would have found his brass ring ridiculous and his curls frivolous, and they would have been suspicious of the peacock feathers and velvets decorating his office. Besides, my parents had the firmly rooted idea that analysts weren't real doctors and at times could even be "shady characters." In their judgment, that office would be the setting of foolishness and danger. The idea that I was doing something that would have alarmed my parents made the analysis both alluring and repugnant. I didn't know at the time that Dr. B. was quite a well-known analyst and that influential people whom my parents respected also respected him and even knew him quite well. I thought he was obscure and totally unknown, someone my friend and I had accidentally come upon in the shadows.

The moment I arrived I would start talking in a great rush, for I thought that was what he expected. I thought if I remained silent, he would remain silent too, and then my presence in the office would be totally meaningless. He would listen and smoke, using an ivory cigarette holder, his ironic, profoundly attentive gaze never faltering. I didn't wonder then whether he was intelligent or stupid, but I realize now that the light of his intelligence shone acutely on me. It was his radiant intelligence that lit my way through that black summer.

I loved talking with him. The word "love" may sound foolish, applied to analysis, which in itself is unlovable, bitter, and painful. And yet I never could see this painful aspect of analysis which others later spoke of. Possibly my analysis was flawed. Without a doubt it was flawed. Now that I recall my impetuous talking, I tend to think I couldn't have been laboriously wrenching secrets out of my soul. Instead I was darting about chaotically, at random, on the trail of some remote point I hadn't yet located. Always I had the feeling that the essential thing still remained to be uttered. I talked so much, yet I never succeeded in telling the whole truth about myself.

It bothered me no end to think that I had to pay him. If my father had known, not only about my analysis but about all the money I was spending on Dr. B., he would have screamed to high heaven. Still, it wasn't so much the idea of my father's screaming that distressed me. It was the idea that I had to pay money for the attention Dr. B. devoted to my words. I was paying for his patience with me. (Although I knew I was the patient, I found him very patient with me.) I was paying for his irony and his smile, for the silence and dimness of his office, for the water and the ice; nothing was given for nothing, and this I found intolerable. I told him so, and he said it was to be expected. He always anticipated everything—I could never take him by surprise. Everything I ever told him about myself he had known for ages, because others had suffered and thought the same things. This was irritating, yet at the same time a great relief, for in my own private thoughts, I sometimes imagined I must be too weird and solitary to have any right to live.

There was another thing, too, that struck me as absurd between me and Dr. B., and that was the unilateral nature of our relationship. The matter of money might make me angry, but this one-sidedness seemed to create a profound and irrevocable discomfort between us. I was obliged to talk about myself, but it would hardly have been appropriate for me to start asking questions about him in turn. I didn't question him because at the moment it didn't occur to me to do so, and also because I felt I had to be as discreet and circumspect as possible about his private life. But as I left his house I used to try to conjure up his wife, the other rooms of his apartment, his life outside of analysis. I felt that something crucial was excluded from our relationship, namely, mutual sympathy. Even the water he gave me each day was not intended for my thirst, but was part of a ritual established God knows where or by whom, and from which neither of us could escape. And this ritual allowed no space for compassion. I wasn't supposed to find out anything about his thoughts or his life. And even if he, scrutinizing my soul and my life, might have felt some compassion, it was the sort of one-sided compassion that receives nothing in return but money, and so cannot in any way resemble true compassion, which always includes the possibility of mutual commitment and response. True, we were patient and doctor. But my illness, if it existed, was an illness of the soul;

the words that passed between us every day were words about my soul, and it seemed to me that such a relationship could not do without reciprocal friendship and sympathy. And still I felt that sympathy and friendship were inadmissible in that office, and that even if a pale ghost of them should appear, it would be only fitting to banish it from our dialogue.

Once he was offended by me, which I found comical. I had met a girl I knew on the street, who was also seeing him (little by little I discovered that lots of people I knew were seeing him). This girl told me that as a writer I was making a mistake undergoing analysis, because though it would heal my spirit, it would kill off every creative faculty. I told this to Dr. B. and he became very red and angry. I had never seen him angry—all I had ever seen in his gaze were the irony and the smile. Pounding his fine white-ringed hand on the table, he told me that it was untrue and the girl was a fool. If I were being analyzed by a Freudian, he said, I might possibly lose the desire to write, but since he was a Jungian this would not happen. Indeed I would write better books if I came to know myself better. He spun out an elaborate explanation of the difference between Jung and Freud. I lost the thread and got distracted, and to this day I don't exactly know what is the real difference between Jung and Freud.

One day I told him that I could never manage to fold blankets symmetrically, which gave me a feeling of inferiority. He left the office for a moment and returned with a blanket, which he folded, holding it under his chin. He wanted me to try to fold it too. I did, and to be obliging I said that I had mastered it, but it wasn't true, because even now I find it difficult to fold blankets evenly.

One night I dreamed that my daughter was drowning and I was saving her. It was a very colorful dream, full of precise details: the lake or sea was a violent blue, and my mother was on the shore wearing a big straw hat. Dr. B. said that in the dream my mother represented my past femininity and my daughter my future femininity. I had always accepted his explanations of my dreams, but this time I rebelled and said that surely dreams didn't always have to be symbolic: I had really dreamed about my daughter and my mother and they didn't symbolize anything at all. I simply missed them, especially my daughter, whom I hadn't seen in months. I think I showed some impatience in contradicting him. That may have been the first sign that my involvement in psychoanalysis was wavering and that I needed to invest my energies elsewhere.

We began to have disputes during the sessions, because I felt I ought to leave Rome and go back north. I thought my children would be better off in Turin where my parents lived and where we could have a home. According to Dr. B. I was mistaken: I should get myself settled in Rome with the children. I outlined all the problems of setting up house in Rome, but he shrugged his shoulders and said I was getting worked up over nothing and not facing my responsibilities. He said I was creating false obligations. Our first real disagreement arose over these true and false obligations. Meanwhile the weather turned cool, and one day I found him wearing a shirt buttoned to the neck and a little bowtie. That bowtie on his austere Jewish body struck me as inane, the most inane sign of frivolity. I didn't even bother to tell him, so pointless had my relationship with him become. I abruptly quit going to him and sent the last payment along with a brief note. I'm sure he was not the least bit surprised and had anticipated it all. I left for Turin and never saw Dr. B. again.

In Turin over the next few months, I would occasionally wake up at night with some nagging notion which might have been useful in analysis and which I had neglected to bring up. I even spoke to myself with a German accent once in a while. Years passed. When I chanced to think of my analysis, it was always as

one of the numerous things I had started and not finished because of my disorganization, ineptitude, and confusion. Much
later, I returned to Rome. I was living right near Dr. B.'s office
and knew he was still there; a couple of times it occurred to me
to drop in and say hello. But our relations had grown from such
a peculiar root that an ordinary visit wouldn't have made any
sense. I felt that the old ritual would immediately begin all over
again—the table, the glass of water, the smile. I couldn't bring
him friendship, I could only bring him the burden of my neuroses. I hadn't freed myself of my neuroses; I had simply learned
to tolerate them, or in the end, had forgotten them. Then one
day I heard that Dr. B. was dead. That was when I regretted
never having seen him again. If there is a place where the dead
meet, surely I shall see Dr. B. there: our talk will be simple, heedless of analysis and neurosis, and maybe even cheerful, tranquil,
and flawless.

March, 1969

the white mustache

When I was eleven years old I learned that I would have to walk to school all by myself. I was plunged into depression by the news, but didn't say a word about it and hid my desolation with a broad, fake smile; I had lately developed the habit of keeping silent and smiling whenever I felt ashamed of myself.

I had never gone out alone and had never gone to school, having completed the elementary grades at home. Teachers came to give me my lessons, teachers my mother would frequently replace because I used to fall asleep: she was always hoping to find one who could keep me awake. The most recent was a young woman with a felt hat. When after a long hesitation I came up with the right answer, she would say only, "Te deum." She said it so fast that it sounded like "tedem," and for a long time I couldn't make out what this word "tedem," whispered through her teeth, might mean. In any event, thanks to Miss Tedem I passed the exams for the elementary school diploma.

My mother informed me that I was now enrolled at the *"ginasio,"* or junior high school. She pronounced "ginnasio" wrong, with only one "n." The *"ginasio"* was where I had taken my exams, and as it was very near my house I would have to go there and return alone, because I had to stop being what I was, namely, "a hopeless case."

[85]

I was a "hopeless case" in various ways. I couldn't dress myself or lace my shoes; I couldn't make my bed or light the gas; I couldn't knit, though the knitting needles had been placed in my hands many times; moreover I was very sloppy and left my things scattered around as if, my mother would say, we had "twenty servants." Meanwhile other girls my age could do laundry, iron, and cook entire meals.

I didn't think that going to school by myself could cure me, at this point, of being "a hopeless case." I would be a hopeless case forever. I'd heard my father declare that I would be a hopeless case forever, not through any fault of my own but because my mother had brought me up all wrong and spoiled me. I too believed it was my mother's fault and not mine, but this was no consolation for not being like those clever, enviable girls who ironed and mended sheets, handled soap and money, locked and unlocked their front doors and took the trolley by themselves. We were and would remain worlds apart. Also, I had no specific talents: I wasn't athletic, I wasn't studious, I wasn't anything. And though I had known this for some time, having heard it repeated often enough at home, it suddenly felt like a terrible misfortune.

Still, my father didn't want me going out alone. The maid was supposed to accompany me to school, since, as he was always saying, "she never did anything anyway." "It's on your head if you send her to school alone," he shouted at my mother, and she assured him that the maid would go with me at all times. She was lying and I knew it. I was aware that my father was told lies now and then; that was necessary, my mother said over and over, because he had "a terrible temper": the lies gave us all a little breathing space in which to arm ourselves against his numerous commands and prohibitions. I had noticed, though, that while my brothers' lies had some chance of survival, my mother's were born sickly, from an inherent weakness, and died out in the space of a day. I myself never lied to my father, simply because I didn't have the courage ever to address a word to him: I lived in holy dread of him. If he happened to ask me something, I answered so faintly as to be inaudible, and he would shout that he couldn't hear me. Then my mother would tell him what I had said, and my words, in my mother's voice, sounded pathetic. I would give that broad, stupid smile, the smile that spread over my face when I quivered with fear and with the shame of my fear.

I was sure my father would promptly discover that no one was taking me to school. As a rule, his anger would lash out at my mother's lies with gale force. I hated being the cause of my parents' quarrels; it was the one thing in the world I hated and feared the most.

Thus far I had led a charmed life, before going to school. It was definitely the life of a hopeless case, but how I loved looking back on it. I would get up late and take long, very hot baths, disobeying my father, who insisted and believed that I took cold baths all year round. I would linger over my fruit and bread, and then settle down to reading, scrunched up on the floor with my piece of bread. Of all the awful catastrophes that might befall me, I often thought, one was that my father might decide to stop working at his institute, where he spent his days in a gray laboratory smock, and instead would bring everything home, his smock, his microscope, and the slides he pored over, and then my entire morning routine would be forbidden, from the hot baths to the bread I nibbled on the floor while I read. I wasn't studious. My father took no interest in my studies since, as he often stated, he had "enough on his mind." He was, on the contrary, preoccupied with the education of one of my brothers, who was a few years older than I and "had no ambition whatsoever," which made my father "lose the gleam in his eye." From time to time my mother would inform him that I "didn't grasp arithmetic," but this information failed to rouse him. Still, as a matter of principle he would thunder against "laziness." My mornings were pure laziness—I knew it and brooded over it as I munched bread and read novels, vaguely guilty and profoundly contented.

When my teacher arrived I stood up bemused, with pins and needles in my knees; I joined her at the table and handed her my unfinished, incorrect homework. She would get angry and yell, but I wasn't afraid; accustomed as I was to my father's rages, Miss Tedem's shouts were like the cooing of doves. I studied her felt hat, her pearls, her silk scarf; neither her chignon speared with tortoiseshell hairpins nor her purse lying on the table, very like my mother's purse, could inspire the least shiver of fear. It was my father's features that evoked terror: his furrowed brow, his freckles, his narrow cheeks, wrinkled and hollowed, his bristling, curly eyebrows, his grim red crew cut.

My life changed abruptly when I started school. I had just learned to tell time—till then I had never needed to know what time it was. Now, when I woke up I checked the clock a million times, both the alarm clock on the night table and the huge clock on the street corner just opposite my window. I hated those two clocks. My life was gradually being taken over by things I hated. On waking, I would roll up the blinds with a vast melancholy, to gaze out at the street that awaited me, still dark and deserted, the clock lit by a dim streetlamp. I had to go to school by myself: thus my mother had decreed. I could have told my father, but I quickly banished that notion in dread. The ensuing storms would overwhelm me. Strangely enough, my mother's lie about the maid going with me held up—one of her rare lies endowed with vital force.

I hated the porcelain washbasin in my room, where I washed carelessly and inadequately, fiddling around with the cold bar of soap; I hated going out in the hall and possibly meeting my father on the days he was late, and hearing his unflattering exclamations about my appearance: my dressing gown, which he found ridiculous, my dazed face, my pallor. He hurled these comments at my mother, who was still in bed and answered in a plaintive stammer. My great worry was that he might linger at home long enough to see me leaving *by myself.* With relief, I would watch him wrap himself in his enormous raincoat, tug his beret down on his fiery crew cut, and slam the glass-paned door on his way out, leaving it to tremble in his wake. In the dining room the light was on, the signs of his passage still evident: the smell of his pipe, the teapot on the table, the little tube of anchovy paste and a piece of gorgonzola on a flowered plate, his chair shoved aside and his napkin tossed against the teacup. I found his habits odious; I couldn't see how he could possibly eat gorgonzola at the crack of dawn. I would swallow two sips of tepid caffelatte; my mother wanted me to "get down something hot" before I went out. The maid gave me a small package containing bread and butter and anchovies, which I stuck in my coat pocket. My mother called that "a little snack" to have during the mid-morning recess.

"Did you get down something hot?" she would ask from bed. I didn't answer; I punished her with a cold silence. I punished her for sending me to school alone, for buying me a leaky fountain pen, for making me wear a coat she considered "still good" and I considered ghastly; I punished her because she said "little snack," because she said "*ginasio*" with only one "n," and because she didn't have a "visiting day" as all my classmates' mothers did, as I had lately discovered to my profound chagrin. I punished her; I left without kissing her good-bye.

"Have something hot before you leave" and "don't talk to anyone on the street" were the two things my mother kept repeating over the course of the day. The street, shrouded in mist, was fittingly silent and hostile. I wanted to run but didn't: I was very early and would have been the first to arrive at school, and besides, I was afraid of looking ridiculous. I walked, carrying my school bag and my atlas. Twenty times my shoelaces came undone and twenty times I stopped to tie them. When I got to the avenue I waited for a long time before crossing, since I could never find the right moment, all the while thinking how if I were run over by a tram, maybe even killed, my mother would lament her gross negligence for the rest of her life. From what I could surmise, it was my sister who had convinced her to send me to school by myself, maybe by telling her I was "such a hopeless case" and had been raised "as cloistered as a nun." I had often heard my sister's harsh criticism of my upbringing. I didn't resent my sister for this: all my resentment was directed at my mother, who had turned me into a hopeless case and then cast me out on the streets.

At school, there was no friendly face to welcome me, for I hadn't yet made any friends. This I found inexplicable. I couldn't tell if my coat was to blame, or my beret, or what. My coat had big green and black checks; my mother said it was English wool, but I couldn't have cared less about English wool: it was old and I'd been wearing it for three years; it was short, so that several inches of my skirt stuck out, but this was true of other girls as well. My yellow angora beret was new and expensive, but possibly comical—I wore it flattened down over one ear. My stockings were all wrong. They were brown, made of ribbed cotton; the other girls wore either short white socks, if they were younger or smaller than I, or else sheer silk stockings. My mother said she didn't like young girls wearing women's stockings and my sister agreed. Still, my ribbed cotton stockings were all wrong because *no one* else wore them; later on I saw one girl wearing them, but she was in another class; in my class *no one* had stockings like that, as I tirelessly repeated to my mother when I got back home. She replied that she had bought several pairs and could hardly "toss them out," a reply that struck me as the height of idiocy.

The only person at school who seemed to notice my existence was the teacher—tall, old, slightly stooped, rosy-cheeked, with a goatee. I idolized him from the very first day, because when my pen rolled near his desk and I went to pick it up, he smiled at me. My love for him was drenched in fear. On occasion he would erupt with rage, screaming because the class was noisy; he pounded his fists on the desk and the ink stand shook. And yet my fear didn't seem to rise from his fits of rage, but from something else, I wasn't sure what. He was totally in charge here: it was his blackboard, his chalk, his map of Italy hanging behind him; those objects poisoned him and he poisoned them: his white linen handkerchief and his goatee exuded terror.

I was aware that he knew my teacher, Miss Tedem, and that she had spoken of me, so perhaps he was kind because I had been "recommended" and not out of genuine liking. Yet his kindness, even if clouded by this suspicion, won me over anyway and comforted me. I made up my mind to study for him. It grieved me that he had to see me alone and friendless at my desk, alone during the lunch break, that every morning he had to gaze out at my isolation. I would have liked to appear triumphant, happy and radiant for him, just as I would have liked to hand in perfect homework. My isolation and my ignorance seemed to merge, forming a single and terribly heavy burden, a combination of guilt and disgrace that I dragged behind me wherever I went and would never be free of.

I came to the conclusion that no one was making friends with me because of the notorious "visiting day." My classmates' mothers each had a specific "visiting day," when they had the other mothers over for tea and cakes while the children played and drank hot chocolate. My mother had no such "visiting day" and had never had one. Her friends turned up at odd times and she received them wherever she happened to be—in her room, or on the balcony, or in the ironing room, where they would sit around the table and chat with the seamstress who came for the day. She rarely served her friends tea. She didn't know my classmates' mothers and showed no interest in meeting them. At school the girls would talk about those afternoons: I heard discussions of the cakes, the hairdos and clothes of the various mothers, the furnishings of the various living rooms, discussions that made me feel totally at a loss. I knew nothing about furniture or hairdos, and besides, neither I nor my mother, alas, would ever be invited to those houses. I wasn't even sure I wanted my mother to take part in the teas, for she might well come out with some sudden shameful revelations—that we weren't religious, or that we were antifascists. I had suffered since earliest childhood from my family's lack of religion, but I had always been quite proud of the fact that we were antifascists. Now this too was coming to feel like one more wretched complication.

Twice a week I had to return to school in the afternoon for gym. The first time, I went to gym wearing my usual clothes, and the gym teacher, an old lady with a huge, shaggy gray hat, told me that I had to come "in uniform." The next time, my mother went to see her and explained that I wasn't enrolled in the Fascist Youth Movement and didn't have a uniform. The teacher told her I still had to wear a black pleated skirt and a white piqué blouse for gym, and said she could find the proper skirt and blouse in a store on Via Bogino, where they sold uniforms for the Fascist Youth. The words "Via Bogino" alarmed and distressed me. My mother went to Via Bogino one morning on her own; she reported that when she asked for the blouse and skirt, the saleswoman said, "For a girl in the Fascist Youth, right?" My mother quickly replied, "No, no, it's for gym class," and the saleswoman gave her a dirty look.

"For a girl in the Fascist Youth, right?" "No, no, it's for gym class," I would mutter to myself angrily. I imagined this exchange inevitably ricocheting from Via Bogino all the way back to my school. With loathing, I put on the black pleated skirt and the piqué blouse: the skirt was exactly the same as the ones my classmates wore on gym days, but my blouse didn't have the Fascist party insignia all the other girls had sewn above the little pocket. My whole life I had longed to fight fascism, to dash through the city with a red flag and to sing, covered with blood, on the barricades. Oddly enough I didn't renounce these dreams, and yet the thought of going into gym class without the insignia, confronting the teacher's sullen face under her huge hat, was a painful humiliation.

The hours spent in gym class were the most dreadful of my life. I couldn't climb up the poles, nor could I jump. I wasn't athletic: at home I had been told time and again that I "wasn't athletic," and now, with the pole before me, I felt I was made of lead. When I was very young I used to go to a gymnastics class—Swedish gymnastics—and I was the best of all. How far away were those happy days! The teacher with the huge hat handed each of us two little barbells to take home so we could exercise there too, in front of the mirror. We were supposed to swing the barbells in a circle and say, "Twirl, twirl, circle, four." What loathsome words! They echoed inside me drearily all day long, relentlessly reminding me of the huge, gray shaggy hat shaped like a cylinder, the sullen mouth that hated me and that I hated, because I turned right when I should have turned left, because I didn't have the insignia, because at the gymnastics display held in the stadium at the end of the year I would disgrace her, as she had warned me. I would heap shame on both our heads.

One morning, as I stood on the avenue waiting for the right moment to cross, a man rose up out of the fog and greeted me. He was a short, rosy-cheeked man with a big drooping white mustache. I mistook him for an acquaintance of my father's, one Professor Sacchetti, who I knew lived in this neighborhood, so I greeted him in return. He took my arm and crossed the street with me. He asked how old I was. Then he asked a very odd question. He asked, "Do you have a papa?" I realized he couldn't possibly be Professor Sacchetti; my father's image suddenly loomed before me, immense and furious. I was walking arm in arm with a stranger. Yet I didn't dare to disengage myself and I kept walking, politely holding his arm. He gave off a strong smell of cologne and he wore gray wool gloves with snaps. A few steps from the door of the school, he raised his hat to me and receded into the fog. One of my classmates, a girl with blonde bangs, asked who was that man I was walking with. I told her I'd never seen him before. Was I out of my mind, she said, walking arm in arm with a total stranger? She said it was wrong of my mother to send me to school all alone. The words "wrong of your mother" wounded me to the core. This girl always came to school with a maid and a cousin. For her mother, the maid hardly counted. She insisted on the cousin as well. I had no girl cousins. I envied everything about this girl, her blonde bangs, her starched collar with the blue ribbon, her great prudence, her father who was an army officer, the inscribed portrait of Prince Umberto in her living room. I'd never seen the portrait, but I had heard it mentioned by girls who'd been to her house.

A bitter remorse swept over me. I had done what my mother always told me not to do. I had "talked to a stranger." I was horrified to recall our conversation, so polite and subdued. I had had several frightening encounters in the past, in the public gardens and at the movies, but right now there was nothing quite so incomprehensible as those gloves with the snaps and that genteel mustache.

I stared at the teacher explaining the lesson: in his rosy cheeks and his wrinkled, white-haired temples I could see some faint resemblance to the man with the white mustache.

The strange thing was that I couldn't possibly tell my mother I had walked and talked with that man. It struck me that my conversations with my mother, since I started going to school, had become so offhand and depleted that they left no room for entire sentences. My tone with her was contemptuous, stinging, and terse. There was simply no way, in that stinging tone, to confess to a mistake or ask for help.

I should have stripped away my scorn. But to strip it away even for a moment was unthinkable—it encased me like a straitjacket. What on earth had happened to me, I wondered. How had I suddenly come to scorn my own mother?

I thought of confiding in my sister. My sister was married and lived in another city, but she sometimes visited on the weekends. She and my mother would sit and talk in the living room, and often my mother would weep: it grieved her that my sister had left home. She felt all alone, old and useless. My sister would comfort her. I felt excluded from all of this; if I came in, they told me to go away. I didn't like seeing my mother weep so often. This, I thought, was what made me scorn her: those tears, which spread insecurity and gloom through my life. If I wished to speak to my sister, I would have to call her into my room. This was far too difficult. I stared straight into my isolation: there wasn't a person in the world I could readily speak to about the white mustache.

I decided I would run to school every day. I saw him there all the time, every morning, standing at the corner, facing the avenue: tranquil, rosy-cheeked, courteous, with his dark overcoat, his silk scarf, his hat raised in greeting. I dashed past him, running like a hare. Panting for breath, I took refuge in the doorway of the school. I would see him again when school was out. Then, after a while, I didn't see him anymore. He disappeared.

But it was as if he had cast a pall over the whole city. He was there, hidden and virulent, lurking on some unknown street with his mustache and his gloves. Sometimes I would say to myself in his courteous, guttural voice, "Do you have a papa? Well, do you?"

Finally I stopped being afraid of him. But he became a symbol of all that was unknown and that filled me with dread. He was everything: he was mathematics, which I didn't understand and which my mother, forever inept, kept calling "arithmetic"; he was the least common denominator and the greatest common multiple; he was my life outside the house, in the fog, far from my mother; he was my isolation, my failure to make friends, my struggles over homework, my sorrow at growing up, the melancholy that assailed me when the city grew dark, when I gazed out the window at the disconsolate nocturnal streets. There was a time when the city had been as lucid and simple as my own home, made up of streets and avenues where I played and chased dogs and caught salamanders to put in a shoebox, where I leaned over the bridge with my mother to watch the boats go by, or leaned over to watch the trains from the overpass. Now, that city I had lived in like a house, like a room, was revealed as unknown, vast and melancholy, all its old bright, merry places inundated and swept away.

I hadn't known sadness, in childhood; I had only known fear. Now I enumerated all the things in my childhood that had frightened me: a film with a man called Chan who sat holding a knife; he used the knife to cut bread, but then he killed someone. It happened that my father often mentioned the chancellor of the University, who was also called Cian and whom he couldn't stand because he was a fascist; every time he said "Cian" I would see the bread and the knife and I would shiver. I was also afraid of the fascists, of their black shirts and the green bands on their legs, their trucks, and the song *Giovinezza, Giovinezza**; and of the Labor Office that was burned down; and of a man's hat covered with blood and dirt I once saw next to a mangled bicycle on a curb; and of a weeping woman running away from a man who pursued her. As a child, all these things had made me suspect that amid the clear light of the universe lurked something dark. And yet they were only fears and could vanish in a trice: all it took was my mother's voice ordering the groceries, or the promise of a special outing, or a guest arriving, or some appetizing new dish appearing on the table, or the sight of our trunks reminding me of summer and going to the country. But now, behind fear stretched depression. It was no longer just a suspicion, it was my constant certainty that the universe wasn't lucid and simple but on the contrary was dark, twisted, and secret; secrets lurked everywhere; streets and people hid grief and evil, and the gloom would never go away; no power could ever vanquish it. Guests could arrive and tasty dishes appear on the table, I could have a new dress, a new book, I could see trunks and dream of trains and summer and the country: wherever I went, gloom would follow. It was always there, immovable, boundless, incomprehensible, inexplicable, like a desolate black sky looming way overhead.

July, 1970

---

* "Youth, Youth."

the great lady

The English novelist Ivy Compton-Burnett, whom Alberto Arbasino* used to call "the great lady," died in London last August. I found this out a few days ago in an article by Arbasino. To say I was sorry to hear of her death might sound foolish: she was, I believe, almost ninety years old, she lived alone, and she must have led a fossil-like existence. And yet the news of her death saddened me. So she is no longer writing her dry, brilliant novels. And I never saw her; now I'll never see her. I wanted so much to meet her, and always envied Arbasino because he knew her and had even visited her two or three times in her London home.

What little I know of her, I know through Arbasino. But I had pictured her exactly as he describes her. Very, very old; very, very small; a shawl wrapped around her knees; her hair tidily arranged "like a little wig" over her wrinkled, freckled forehead; her shriveled hands icy and stiff with arthritis; and on a stool beside her, a basket from which she plucked leaves of lettuce at tea time, nibbling them "like a little turtle." Thus Arbasino saw her and thus she must have been for many years; indeed maybe

---

* Italian novelist and critic

[99]

she had been that way forever. A cross between a small bird, a mouse, and a turtle.

There were no men in her life, and no children. According to the brief biographical notes on her book jackets, she lived first with a brother, then with a woman friend. When those two were gone she was alone. The life of an old unmarried English lady: it's easy to imagine. Tea, embroidered doilies, coal, the mail slid under the door, the coin-operated "launderette" once a week; a dignified, well-ordered solitude, a genteel, minimal existence. Yet all the while she was writing those novels. She said of herself, "I started out writing the way I wanted to, feeling that that was my style, and later on I found no reason to change."

She wrote a great many novels, all so much alike that it's difficult to single out and recall any one in particular: complex, meticulous mechanisms that, taken as a whole, form an immense, tortuous structure. She was rather like a clear-sighted, industrious engineer.

In childhood she lived in the country, surely in one of those houses to be found in her novels, jammed with children, dogs, cats, and servants; spacious, uncomfortable, ancient, badly heated by scanty fires, and nestled in a verdant, rainy countryside. Houses where, in her novels, people are consumed by secret incestuous passions and murder infants and burn wills. Yet not a single cry breaks the silence, not a single drop of blood stains the walls. The landscape is the English countryside, thickly settled yet reclusive and lonesome; cultivated yet desolate; wooded, boundless, and somber. Nature and places are invisible in her novels, since she never spends a single syllable describing them; they're invisible, but we feel them all around us as if she had drawn them in detail.

Once in a great while she may linger an instant to describe her characters, but barely, in passing, with only a few brief strokes. It's not haste or lack of patience that makes Compton-Burnett so rarely pause to describe faces and places; it is rather a disdainful frugality, a fastidious rejection of anything superfluous. The pace of her writing is neither slow nor swift, but the even, precise, and inexorable pace of one who knows just where she has to go. Her patience is relentless, infernal.

I discovered her novels about ten years ago, during a period when I was living in England. I stumbled upon them by chance. Reading one for the first time, I had the unpleasant sensation of being caught in a trap. I felt pinned to the ground. I looked for them everywhere. I don't know much English; I read those novels with extreme difficulty, and every so often I wondered why on earth I so stubbornly and laboriously persisted in reading a writer I might well detest.

At first, reading her novels, I seemed to be moving through a landscape of fog. I couldn't quite tell if the fog came from the fact that I understood English with difficulty, or if the fog shrouding those wintry places was genuine, created by the author. They are novels made up almost entirely of dialogue; through the fog I could hear the measured beats of the dialogues striking, bouncing from one point to another, dry and precise as Ping-Pong balls. At that point, I hadn't been writing for quite some time, and suddenly I felt something reawaken in me that had been long dormant: those precise, dry sounds suddenly and imperiously brought me back to the lost path.

And still I kept telling myself that I didn't like her novels at all and might even loathe them; they evoked things so remote and alien to me: a Ping-Pong game, a chess game, a geometrical theorem. Then all at once I realized that in fact I loved them wildly; I took joy and comfort in them; I could drink them in like water from a fountain—no matter that they were dry and airless. There wasn't any kind of fog, I was mistaken about the fog; on the contrary, a dazzling clarity, naked and inexorable, suffused them, and in this inexorable clarity, impenetrable creatures sat riveted in their ruthless conversations, exchanging words like serpents' bites. Yet no tears or blood or sweat ever flowed, nor did the characters ever grow pale, maybe because they were already very pale; the wounds produced a piercing but dull grief, and even this was immediately engulfed by new serpent bites. In such a world, no happiness of any kind was possible; for such creatures, happiness didn't exist even as a lost realm; happiness could only take the shape of a grim triumph of money or pride.

I could never grasp where, in such novels, the poetry might reside, and yet I felt it must be somewhere if, dry and airless as they were, one could breathe and drink them in, and feel, in their midst, a profound, comforting and redeeming happiness. Then I understood that poetry was present the way nature was present: the poetry, totally invisible, totally unwilled, neither offered nor intended for anyone, was there in the same way as the dull, limitless sky that stretched behind those malicious, isolated strokes. And so a diligently constructed mechanism was miraculously transformed into something in which any casual observer could recognize his own face and his own fate.

While I was spending my days in London reading her novels *Mother and Son, Brothers and Sisters, Elders and Betters, A God and His Gifts,* I was always hoping to meet Ivy Compton-Burnett walking down the street. I had been told she lived in my neighborhood. So I studied all the little old ladies walking up and down the avenues. One day I went to a brunch I had heard she was invited to. She didn't show up. She talked only of trivia anyway, my hosts said; her conversation was of no interest. But I didn't care anything about her conversation. I simply wanted to see her, and to tell her somehow, in my crude and meager English, how immensely important her books had been to me.

Of course she would have found me absurd. Someone like me could only have struck her as absurd—gratuitous and sentimental. She would have found words like gratitude or love for her books quite superfluous. She was probably as completely unegotistical as a turtle or an engineer: in that lay her greatness. Still, I would have liked, if only for an instant, to live in her field of vision. As far as her conversation being trivial, as they claimed, that didn't surprise me. Surely she wouldn't waste any words in social chit chat; for ordinary conversation, she would dole out a suitably ordinary voice, a trifling, querulous whisper, just as she would dole out a few coins to buy her newspaper, counting them in her worn-out glove. Maybe she released her real voice, loud, violent, and tragic, only in the dark recesses of her soul.

December, 1969

a place to live

Years ago, when our apartment in Turin was sold, we decided to look for a place in Rome, and this search for a home took a very long time.

For years I had longed for a house with a garden. As a child in Turin, I had lived in a house with a garden, and I envisioned and longed for a house just like that one. I wouldn't have been contented with some meager little garden; I wanted trees, a stone fountain, shrubs, paths—everything that had been in the garden of my childhood. Reading the ads in the *Messaggero* every Thursday and Sunday, I lingered over the ones that said, "villa with ample garden, two thousand square meters, tall old trees," but when I called the number in the ad, I would find that the "villa" cost thirty million lire. We didn't have thirty million lire. Then again, sometimes the voice on the other end of the line would say, "thirty million, negotiable," and that word, "negotiable," meant I needn't give up completely on those two thousand square meters of garden, which I wouldn't have dared to go and look at but which I pictured as splendid. "Negotiable" seemed like a slippery slope down which one might slide to the sum, far less than thirty million, which we possessed. I went through the ads in the *Messaggero* religiously every Thursday and Sunday, skipping over all the ones beginning with "Aaaaa"; I'm not sure why, I just didn't trust all those "a's." Not that I didn't trust real-estate agencies. I would have consulted them too, and in fact I did consult several. Still, I skipped over the "aaa's." Since I wanted a garden, that is, a ground-floor apartment, I also skipped over the ads that began with "penthouse," "huge pent-house," "panoramic view." I pounced on those that started with "villa," "villino," "villinetto."* "Villa, residential neighborhood, diplomats' choice, exceptional details, huge garden," or, "elegant villa, stately, for discriminating buyers, actors, professionals, industrialists. Individual thermostat. Lushly wooded park." After seeing two or three "villinetti" and finding them quite bleak, the gardens nothing but a narrow strip of pavement fenced in by a hedge, I took to avoiding the "villinetti" and instead underlined the "villas" with my pencil. "Ten-room villa, large living room, fully tiled patio, central heating, wooded garden." "Three-story villa, large park, ideal for diplomatic headquarters or religious community, bargain." I even lingered for a moment on ads for houses or land outside of Rome, imagining we might set up house in the country. "Frosinone area, bargain, stone quarry, on road with olive grove above, excellent buy." My husband cast his eye over the ads I'd underlined and asked what we would possibly want with a villa suitable for a religious community, seeing that we hardly constituted a religious community, and especially what would we want with a "stone quarry" near Frosinone, seeing that what we required was an apartment in Rome.

At first my husband abstained from the search and watched me underlining ads as if I were possessed by some mild form of madness. He would say that after all he was quite content in the rented apartment we were living in, though he had to grant we were a trifle cramped. Nevertheless he would sometimes admit,

* Private house with garden, cottage, small cottage

albeit half heartedly, that this might be an opportune moment to buy an apartment, since paying rent was throwing money out the window. However, I must emphasize that in the early days my search was a solitary one, and slightly mad; I would read the ads in the *Messaggero* aloud and he would listen, usually in an ironic and scornful silence that was discouraging yet at the same time pushed me ever further along the path of madness. Since buying a house without his assent was impossible, I was pursuing impossible dreams and shadows, knowing there would never be any real consequences. I even went to look at some of the advertised places, and my husband knew I was going, but he refused to join me; instead I was accompanied, on these expeditions, by his total lack of faith in my ability to find a home. Then, on the spur of the moment, my husband started looking with me. This unexpected decision came about, I believe, after he consulted a brother-in-law who advised him that it would be extremely unwise to buy a place just then because in a few years the real-estate market would go down—a prediction that proved erroneous, since the price of apartments in Rome has been rising steadily. It would make sense, therefore, to wait until the market went down. I had often had occasion to note that my husband would consult that brother-in-law in order to do exactly the opposite of what he suggested, never ceasing all the while to praise his relative's great shrewdness and sagacity, and to insist that he be consulted in every circumstance of a financial and practical nature, that is, in everything in which my husband felt himself lacking. In the meantime, my father was writing me constantly from Turin urging us to buy an apartment or, as he expressed it, "permanent quarters," a term that in the archaic language he was inclined to use, particularly in his correspondence, signified an apartment. In the rented apartment that was too cramped for us, we currently had the cleaning woman sleep-

ing in the dining room, which my father found unhygienic, and
one of the children sleeping in the study, which my father found
highly inappropriate. As for my sister-in-law, she tried to dis-
suade us from moving because our present rented apartment
had yellow floors, which, she claimed, gave off a light that was
very flattering to the complexion. Her advice, if we were really
set on buying an apartment, was to convince the landlord to sell
us this one, a solution which, as we had attempted many times
to explain, was unfeasible, since the landlord no more wished to
sell it than we, for various reasons, wished to buy it.

So our search had two phases: the first, in which I searched
on my own, fervently yet timidly, with no self-confidence, because my husband's mistrust and lack of confidence were con-
tagious and because I always require someone else's approval in
any undertaking of a practical nature. And then the second
phase, in which my husband went house-hunting with me.
When he began to accompany me, I found that the kind of
home he had in mind had nothing whatsoever in common with
what I had in mind. I found that he, too, longed for a place like
the one in which he'd spent his childhood. Since our childhoods
had been totally dissimilar, our differences were insurmountable.
I, as I said, wanted a place with a garden: a ground-floor apartment
surrounded by greenery, ivy, trees, even if it was a little dark. He,
having grown up partly on Via dei Serpenti and partly in Prati,
was drawn to apartments in those two areas. He couldn't have
cared less about trees or greenery. He wanted to look out the
window and see rooftops, ancient, peeling walls gnawed by time,
patched sheets flapping over damp alleyways, mossy roof tiles,
rusty gutter pipes, chimney pots, bell towers. So we began to
quarrel because he rejected all the apartments I liked—they
were too expensive or they had some defect. Since he too was
reading the ads now, he would underline with his pencil only

those apartments that were in the center of Rome. He would
come with me to see the places I was interested in, but even before
he started up the stairs, his face was set in such a frown, his silence
was so hostile and contemptuous, that I felt that to induce him
to take a humane look around or exchange a few polite words
with the porter or landlord who was leading the way and opening the shutters, was an impossible task. I told him how much I
hated the way he treated those poor porters and landlords, who
weren't in the least to blame if he didn't like their apartments,
and after this observation of mine he became extremely polite
and ceremonious with the porters and the landlords, almost
obsequious, exhibiting a keen interest in their apartments; he
peered into every closet and even talked about what repairs
would be needed. The first few times I was taken in by this and
thought maybe he did like the place we were looking at just a bit,
but it wasn't long before I caught on that his courteous demeanor
was meant ironically for me; not in his wildest dreams would he
buy the apartment in question.

I remember every dismal detail of certain places that appealed to me: a few decrepit houses in Monteverdevecchio, tar-
nished with age, in a state of profound neglect: their damp little
gardens, their long dark corridors and wrought-iron lamps giving off a faint light, their tiny sitting rooms with stained-glass
windows where little old ladies sat holding hand-warmers, their
kitchens with smelly sinks. And the dismal details of certain
apartments that appealed to him: a trail of rooms as big as barns,
with brick floors and whitewashed walls, clumps of tomatoes
hanging from the ceiling, Turkish-style toilets, narrow balconies
facing courtyards as deep and damp as wells, terraces heaped
with piles of rotting rags. Obviously our taste in apartments had
nothing at all in common. There was, however, one kind of
apartment that we both detested. We both detested, and to the

same degree, the semi-new, sumptuous, and sterile-looking apartments in Parioli, which looked out over streets without a single shop, frequented only by flocks of "nurses" in blue veils pushing fragile black baby carriages that resembled insects; and we both hated the houses in the Vescovio area, crammed together in a tangle of streets and piazzas full of delicatessens and drugstores, covered outdoor markets and webs of trolley tracks. We went to see these apartments we detested anyway. We went because by that point we were both under the demonic sway of the search; we went in order to loathe them even more, for that instant of dread, picturing ourselves exiled in Parioli like goldfish in a bowl, or staring out at those little balconies that looked like flower baskets. Worn out, we would go home to our rented apartment with the yellow floors and ask ourselves if we really cared all that much about moving. In fact we didn't much care. After all, we were getting along well enough where we were. I knew every spot and crack in the walls of that apartment, I knew the dark halos that had formed above the radiators; I knew the clang of the iron slabs that got tossed down at the front door, since our landlord had his workshop adjacent to the door: when we went to pay the rent, he welcomed us amid the flares of his blowtorch and the drone of engines. Each time we paid the rent, our landlord looked surprised; he seemed to have forgotten, each time, that he had rented us the apartment; he barely recognized us, though he was always very cordial; he was utterly engrossed in his shop, and by the arrival of those iron slabs that landed on the pavement with a clanging thump. I had dug a little burrow for myself in that apartment, a burrow where I could hide out like a sick dog when I was sad, drinking my tears, licking my wounds. It was as comfortable as an old shoe. Why move? Any new apartment would feel unfriendly; I'd feel sick living there. All the apartments we had seen and, for a few brief moments, entertained the notion of buying paraded before me as in a nightmare. They all made me feel sick. We'd thought of buying them, but the moment we had decided against it we felt a deep relief, a sense of lightness, like someone who has miraculously escaped a mortal risk.

Could it be that any apartment, any one at all, might eventually become a burrow? Would any place eventually welcome me into its dim, warm, reassuring, kindly light?

Or could it be, rather, that I didn't want to live in any of them, any one at all, because what I really hated wasn't the apartments but myself? Wasn't it true that all the apartments, every last one of them, would do fine, so long as anyone but me was living in them?

Finally we put our own ad in the *Messaggero*. We argued endlessly about its contents. In the end it read as follows: "Seeking apartment in Prati or Monteverdevecchio, five rooms, walk-out terrace or garden." My husband was the one who wanted the words "walk-out terrace," because he loved terraces and, as gradually was becoming clear, hated gardens: he said gardens were always full of dust and rubbish from the balconies above. So my dream of a garden was shattered: clouds of dust would assail those "tall, sturdy plants," those shady paths cherished in my fantasies. Several people answered our ad, but the apartments they were offering weren't anywhere near Prati or Monteverdevecchio and had nothing resembling a "walk-out terrace" or garden. We went to see them anyway. For more than a week after the ad appeared, our telephone kept ringing with offers of apartments. One evening the phone rang around ten o'clock; I answered and heard a stranger's voice, a hearty, emphatic, triumphant male voice saying:

"Hello! This is Commander Piave!* I have a gorgeous apartment in Piazza della Balduina! It's fantastic! There's an inter-

---

* Honorific title granted by the President of the Republic for special contributions in various fields.

com! There's a black alabaster column in the master bath, with mosaics of green fish! When are you coming to have a look? Call me, if I'm not here my wife will answer! There's an intercom! Your husband drives home at one o'clock, the doorman rings to tell you to start the spaghetti boiling! There's a garage too! When are you coming? My wife and I would be delighted to meet you, we'll have tea, I'll drive you to the apartment. I have a Spider! My wife doesn't drive, I've been driving for seventeen years, I had the apartment built for my daughter but she moved to São Paolo in Brazil, my son-in-law is from Brazil, he's in the textile business, they met in Fregene. I have a house in Fregene too, a little gem, that one's not for sale, why would I want to sell it, my wife and I go there every weekend. I have a Spider!"

I had lived in Rome for many years but I still didn't know where Piazza della Balduina was. I consulted my husband and he said he hated that neighborhood.

There were three or four apartments we were on the verge of buying. As a rule, our desire to buy a place lasted two weeks. During those two weeks we went to look at it constantly, at all hours of the day: we tipped the porters and made friends with them; we brought our children along, then my sister-in-law, and finally the brother-in-law whose great wisdom my husband boasted of. We had to beg our children to come; they claimed they didn't care anything about apartments, and they had grave doubts about whether we'd ever buy one—they thought we couldn't make up our minds. My sister-in-law mostly paid atten-tion to the floors: one loose tile, for instance, would determine her negative judgment on the condition of the apartment as a whole. As far as the brother-in-law, he would generally station himself in the entryway, standing stern and erect, swaying back and forth on his heels, with one hand under the lapel of his jacket and one finger rhythmically tapping his chest, and from there he would scrutinize the walls; his opinion of all the apartments was invariably negative, especially at the prospect of our buying one, but he managed to find different, though always alarming, drawbacks in every instance. Either he knew from his connections that the builders were unreliable, or he knew a skyscraper would be put up right across the street and would totally block our view; or he knew the whole neighborhood was slated for immediate demolition—the owners would be dispossessed and forced to move; and in any event there wasn't a single place he didn't find dark, damp, poorly constructed and malodorous. He maintained that the only places we should even consider were those built twenty years earlier—not before and not after. Those were precisely the ones we didn't like.

The first house we seriously considered buying was located near Viale Trastevere. Later on, thinking back, we used to call it "Montecompatri," because it was at the top of a sort of hill and my husband would say the air up there was very pure. "Did you notice," he'd say, "how the air up there feels almost like being in Montecompatri?" "Montecompatri" was a new house, never lived in. It stood straight up over a precipice, a wooded ravine that went all the way down to the avenue at a point where it widened into an open space where an amusement park had been built. Now, some years later, the wooded ravine is gone, as is the amusement park. Now nothing remains but houses, so that when I pass by, I can't even recognize the one we wanted to buy, tall and narrow as a tower, looking out over empty space. It had a terrace and a huge living room with large windows opening onto that wild green chasm, and we would often go there at sunset, when the panorama was solemn and desolate, with the city flashing in the distance amid fiery clouds. The house was owned by an agency whose phone number was written on a card stuck on a pole in the middle of the green chasm, but the phone was always either busy or didn't answer. The porter told us to keep trying, which we did regularly, but with no success. The porter was very kind and sympathetic, and seemed eager for us to buy the house. One day we went there resolved to buy it. It was three o'clock on a summer afternoon and the sun was beating straight down on the red-hot tiles of the terrace; a strong odor of garbage rose up from the ravine; as a matter of fact there was a mound of garbage, which we'd never really noticed until just then, baking in the grass under the sun, a few meters above the amusement park. The amusement park was silent and deserted, with its huge, motionless Ferris wheel and rides and lowered awnings; off in the distance, the city was baking against a blinding blue sky. The panorama might be stupendous, I thought, but it inspired thoughts of suicide.

So we fled that house for good. My husband realized the staircase was just too awful, he told me, precious and pretentious; also, that enormous black and gold spider in the entrance hall, two steps from the friendly porter's booth—he couldn't have tolerated the sight of that black spider every day.

After that, we were charmed by two identical attached houses that were both for sale. They were right off Piazza Quadrata, an area my husband loathed. I, on the contrary, loved the area around Piazza Quadrata because I had lived there many years back, before I met my husband or even knew he existed; the Germans were occupying Rome and I was hiding in a convent in that neighborhood. It felt as if all the places I loved in Rome were where at some point in my life I had put down roots, where I had suffered and considered suicide, and walked the streets not knowing which way to turn.

One of the two identical houses near Piazza Quadrata had a garden. What my husband liked most in this house was an inside staircase leading to a basement with a very large kitchen and a long, narrow dining room; in general, when we had some feel-

ing for a house, we would constantly dwell on all the rooms and
features we liked and try to ignore everything else. Thus, my
husband kept going up and down that polished mahogany staircase, which he thought of as "British style." He went up and
down, stroking the banisters as if they were a horse's rump. We
both admired the kitchen, which had cheerful little tiles with
blue flowers. For love of the staircase and the kitchen, we were
inclined to overlook the fact that for our purposes, it was a room
short: we would have to put in a partition to create a small bed-
room in the hall. And my husband seemed to have forgotten
how much he hated the neighborhood, as well as what he had
always said on the subject of gardens—how rubbish and dust
rained down from the balconies above. There was a small statue
in the garden, draped in ivy, and a pergola with stone benches;
we thought we might build a little gazebo in the center of the
garden, where one of the children could sleep, thereby solving
the problem of the missing room. The house next door didn't
have a proper garden, only a narrow strip of greenery: what we
liked best in that house was a room with a bowed window looking out on the garden of the other house. The room had white
gilded furniture, which was very lovely, but of course the landlord would be taking it away: we'd always linger in that room because we liked it and were trying to figure out if we would like it
as much without the furniture, or with our banal, nondescript
furniture. Then we tried to figure out whether we would rather
look down at the garden from that beautiful bowed window or
look up at the bowed window from the shelter of the pergola.
Wouldn't it be wonderful, I said, if we could buy both houses?
My husband pointed out that we couldn't even afford to buy one
of them. I was crazy, he said, a megalomaniac. We argued
fiercely over those two houses. It wasn't that either of us had a
strong preference for either house: no, we both had grave doubts,
and we each accused the other of being unable to decide, besides

which, my husband started in all over again about how he had loathed the neighborhood around Piazza Quadrata from earliest childhood. Our children, when consulted, said that they too loathed that area, but that they wanted to sleep in the gazebo in the garden, the gazebo that didn't yet exist but which they were fighting over, each one wanting it for himself. Then my sister-in-law came with us one day to see the house with the garden, but we happened to go on a morning when the living-room floors were being taken up and tarred, and from the way the tar was being applied my sister-in-law could tell instinctively that those floors would never be quite right, they would always give us trouble and aggravation, and she firmly advised against our buying that house, and by extension the other house as well, which we couldn't see that day, but whose floors, my sister-in-law said, must be just as bad.

After a phase in which I hated every apartment in Rome, I went through a phase in which I felt I loved them all, so much so that I couldn't possibly choose one. Then, when it was clear we wouldn't be buying the house with the bowed window or the house with the pergola, I started hating them all again. In the meantime I was getting letters from my father that inevitably began: "I must advise you that it would be wise to make up your mind to purchase permanent quarters."

And from time to time the phone would ring and we heard the usual hearty, emphatic voice: "Hello! This is Commander Piave! You haven't yet come to see my apartment in Piazza della Balduina! It's fantastic! The windowsills are all black onyx and the living-room floors are marble! There's an intercom! I could even give you some plants for the living room, my wife has a really stunning pink azalea! My wife is wild about plants!"

There was yet another house we were on the point of buying. It was a house with absolutely nothing to recommend it except its low cost. This one, too, was near Viale Trastevere, on a hilly street which, after about a twenty-minute walk, led to the Janiculum Hill. "Do you realize it's only a few minutes from the Janiculum?" my husband would say, in praise of the house. But you couldn't see the Janiculum from the windows; indeed you couldn't see anything from the windows, not a thing except a sheet-metal roof and a blank yellowish wall, a few other buildings neither high nor low, and the street. The street was quiet and usually fairly deserted. The house had two floors: a "villinetto." It was between a mattress-maker and a wine shop. It had a gray front door with a knocker. It had a terrace with a withered arbor. It was neither new nor old, a house without age or character. You went through the gray front door into a hallway with marbled tiles, and made your way up a large staircase with a bulging banister; on the ground floor were a kitchen, a bathroom and a storeroom where the landlord had stacked a collection of chairs; on the floor above was a series of rooms, neither large nor small, strung along a corridor with marbled tiles. All the rooms looked out on the street, that hilly street that did in fact lead to the Janiculum but seemed rather to go nowhere, an aimless street that felt arbitrary and forgotten; a peculiar street, my husband said, and yet one day it might become very important, a crucial artery linking the Janiculum and Viale Trastevere, in which case if we were to buy that house, we might very well suddenly find ourselves in a critical location, one of the most sought-after locations in the city, and then that house we had bought very cheaply would so sharply increase in value that we could resell it for more than twice what we paid. But if we have to resell it, I said, then why buy it? We'd just have to start looking all over again.

It wasn't only the street that was strange—though not unappealing, my husband said; the house was somewhat strange too, though not unappealing. The entrance, well, no, the entrance was hideous, those fake marble tiles were truly ghastly. The staircase wasn't half bad. And the terrace wasn't too bad either. ("You have to imagine a lush green arbor in place of that dried-out arbor. Just picture it. You have no imagination.") We didn't bring anyone to see that house. We didn't talk about it with any enthusiasm. We might have been a little ashamed of it.

Then one day, strolling around the city, we saw a For Sale sign tacked to a door. We went in. And that was how we found our apartment.

It was right in the center of the city. My husband liked it because it was centrally located and because it was on the top floor and looked out over rooftops. He liked it because it was old, big, and massive; it had old ceilings with huge beams which in certain rooms were covered with travertine. It was the first time I had ever heard him mention travertine. Why did I like it? I don't know. It wasn't on the ground floor but on the top floor. It had no garden and there wasn't a tree for miles around. It was stone in the midst of stone, squeezed between chimney pots and bell towers. But maybe I liked it because it was right near an office I used to work in many years ago, before I met my husband; the Germans had just left Rome and the Americans had arrived. I used to go to that office every day. Every day, for superstitious reasons, I would put my foot in an indentation in the pavement, an indentation in the shape of a foot. That indentation was right in front of a little gate. I'd open the gate and go up a small staircase. The office was on the second floor and overlooked an old courtyard with a fountain. The fountain, the little gate, and the indentation in the sidewalk were just a stone's throw from the apartment we saw one morning, my husband and I, and when we walked out, we were resolved to live there. The fountain, the courtyard, the little gate and the indentation in the sidewalk were still there, but the office was no more. The rooms where the office had once been had returned to what they were before the war, namely, the home of an old countess. But it was still a spot in the city that I could recognize as friendly, a place where I had once carved out a little burrow. Not that I had been happy in that office; as a matter of fact I was desperately unhappy there. But I had carved out a little burrow, and the memory of that burrow of years ago kept me from feeling like a stranger who had just happened upon those streets and alleys by mistake. So the idea of that apartment wasn't oppressive to me.

Everyone advised against it. They said any place that old was sure to have lots of problems, leaky pipes, hidden cracks. They said it was bound to rain in on us. They said there would certainly be cockroaches ("beetles," as my sister-in-law put it. Whenever we talked about buying an old place she would hastily say, "but watch out for beetles!"). All in all, they said every bad thing possible about that apartment. They said it would be cold in winter and hot in summer. Some of the things they said proved true. It was true that it rained in on us and we had to have the roof fixed. I found only one cockroach. I sprayed a little insecticide in its wake and it never turned up again. Now we live here and can't tell anymore if the apartment is ugly or beautiful. We feel like we've burrowed in. It fits us like an old shoe. We've stopped thinking about apartments altogether. The words "walk-out terrace," "individually regulated thermostat," "five rooms," "very sunny," "down payment with mortgage," "partial financing acceptable," have dropped out of our vocabulary. But for a good while after we started the moving preparations, after we started the series of complicated investigations regarding walls, pipes, and water tanks and the involved negotiations with metalworkers, electricians, and carpenters, every now and then the phone would ring in the apartment we were about to vacate, which was full of trunks, wrapping paper, and straw. The phone would ring and we'd hear the familiar hearty, triumphant voice:

"Hello! This is Commander Piave! When are you coming to see my apartment in Piazza della Balduina? It's so fantastic! There's an intercom! The doorman lets you know your husband is on his way, you throw the spaghetti in the pot, he puts the car in the garage, rides up in the elevator, and lunch is on the table! There's a black alabaster column in the bathroom with mosaics of fish. All the windowsills are onyx! All you have to do is call, you'll have tea with my wife, I'll come and take you right there, you can rest a while on the belvedere, what a great view of Rome, the whole panorama, we'll have a drink, I'll drive you back in no time at all! I have a Spider!"

October, 1965

clueless travelers

There are people who know how to travel, and others who don't. There are people for whom the slightest trip, or prospect of a trip, means anxiety and fatigue, an exhausting project. For others, it's as simple as blowing their nose.

Not that those who can't travel may not find some subtle pleasure in their rare trips, but it is a pleasure so blanketed in mist that they don't even notice it; only later, in retrospect, do they glimpse its shadow. Nor is it a pleasure that springs from discovering or having discovered new places; these clumsy travelers are sedentary creatures who don't feel any genuine, tranquil curiosity about new places. What they seek from a new place is solely the opportunity to live there as though it might be forever, to transform the new place into a permanent abode. The pleasure of traveling, for them, consists simply of the pungent, dizzying sensation of imagining their life taking place somewhere other than its usual setting.

It is hard to enumerate the anxieties of those who don't know how to travel, anxieties that keep them in a state of alarm for days on end, and come swooping down at the moment of departure. First of all, they're afraid of missing the train or the plane—a fear they find strange, since it is in direct contrast to their deep desire, which is to stay at home. Then, they're afraid of getting on the wrong train or plane and ending up God knows where; of having left behind some essential item; of having brought the wrong clothes and packed the suitcases all wrong; of having locked the suitcases and lost the key. Finally, they're afraid the suitcases will get lost. Recalling what was in them, they're surprised to be fearing their loss, since the contents seem nothing but a wretched jumble of wrong choices.

In a flash of lucidity, they realize that all their fears are merely clouds gathering in a sky emptied of thought. They have in fact suddenly lost every faculty of coherent thought. They don't remember what on earth might have driven them to go away, yet they no longer wonder why they're going, since by this point they are incapable of posing sensible questions or addressing themselves in a human tongue. Their head holds nothing but a clutter of chaotic words—advertising slogans and the refrains of songs that echo insistently in a mental vacuum, whirling and bouncing around mockingly in the void.

Once they arrive in the foreign city, these clueless travelers take refuge in a hotel, this hotel signifying not a point from which to set out and see the city, but truly a refuge in which to hide and cower, the way cats or mice cower under a sofa. The hotel room, for them, is no simple hotel room, temporary and of no intrinsic interest, but a real residence, at once reassuring and hostile, protective and repugnant. Like a stepmother's lap, it is loveless—yet all the same it provides the only warmth life can offer. They pass long hours there, unable to tear themselves away. As if poised at the edge of an abyss, they gaze down with a fascinated dread at the hotel courtyards, gloomy and dark as wells, with snaking black iron stairs and gutter pipes. They are quite aware that beyond those courtyards lies the lovely city, graced by boulevards, trees, museums, and theaters, the city which others in their place would be rushing out to explore without wasting a single instant. They're quite aware of that, and yet they can't manage to tear themselves away from their bleak contemplation of those gutter pipes. Now and then they remind themselves that they supposedly made this trip for pleasure.

When they get thirsty they drink lukewarm tap water, so as not to bother the hotel by asking for mineral water or ice, just in case the hotel might be unable to provide this and would suffer embarrassment. Clueless travelers can't seem to grasp that the hotel is different from a home. They can't see it as an automatic, impersonal world. It is very hard for them to keep in mind that they have to pay for staying there. When it does come to mind, that too is a source of anxiety, for they're never sure if they brought along enough money.

Besides, in foreign countries, clueless travelers have the sense that they couldn't possibly use that unfamiliar money. It doesn't seem like real money. Similarly, the newspapers don't seem real either. They spend hours stretched out on the bed leafing through these unreal newspapers; in the entertainment section they may even find films or plays they've wanted to see for years. But here in this unknown city, they're not sure they still want to—all their curiosity, intelligence, and eagerness to learn new things have glazed over and stultified.

What finally induces them to go out is not the eagerness of discovery but the idea that the hotel staff must be astonished that they never leave their room. With a smile, they consult the concierge. They ask directions and even accept a street map, not that they have any hope of finding their way around—these sedentary creatures have no sense of direction whatsoever and maps mean nothing to them—but so that the concierge who presides over a switchboard and rows of keys hanging alongside him will think they are real tourists who have come to explore the city.

Roaming through the streets, focusing on nothing in particular, their fingers crumpling the map they wouldn't dream of consulting, they are seized by the urge to purchase every object displayed in the store windows. Only by means of these objects, they think, can they somehow take possession of the city. They envision furnishing a house with the old china and the enormous pendulum clocks they see in the antique shops, a house they happened upon while wandering down some side street. In fantasy, they buy heaps of blankets, refrigerators, whole kitchens; they dress up in shawls, furs, hats. They recall their own country as a wasteland, some remote province lacking warm clothes and real wool blankets.

They feel a keen envy for all those people striding by with confidence, obviously knowing exactly where they're going, while their own state of idleness is so humiliating that even their own country suddenly seems uninhabitable—after all, so many people don't live there but here instead, resolute and masterful in this unfamiliar city.

Possessing very slow reflexes, these sedentary creatures follow the tracks of habit, not sensation. They will be open to sensations only when they are no longer called upon to feel them, once the veil of habit has been spread over their surroundings. Born emigrés or refugees, perhaps, these inept travelers cannot transform themselves into tourists. And the strange thing is that though they didn't wish to leave home, now they don't want to return, for they have a faint suspicion that in their absence, something alien and unfriendly may have infiltrated their once familiar haunts.

In the end, they go into a store and buy a dusty eggcup. They regret it at once, as they realize that every corner store in every out-of-the-way town or village in their own country sells identical dusty eggcups.

November, 1969

the baby who saw bears

Three years ago I went to America for the first time in my life. One of my sons had been living there for a year and my grandson was born there. My son, his wife and the baby would be staying another year. The baby was already several months old and I had never seen him except in photographs. And so I was introduced to America and my grandson Simone at the same time. I can't claim to have seen and understood much about America since my responses are slow and I'm not good at grasping new places quickly. What I recall of my trip is this: the afternoon was extremely prolonged, with the plane, apparently motionless, whirring above the white, rounded peaks of clouds in an intensely blue sky where the sun had no intention of sinking. Then all at once came night and rain. That instant when the motionless, glorious afternoon was transformed into a nocturnal storm must have been very swift since I have no recollection of it. When we landed, the wind was raging and covered walkways had been set up on the landing field, the rain pelting down on their zinc roofs.

The first things I saw were streets lashed by the thunderstorm and long, very brightly lit, rumbling underpasses. The city was Boston. Over the course of my life I had read a great many books that told of Boston, but for some unknown reason the only one that came to mind just then was a novel called *The Lamplighter*, which I had read and loved at the age of nine. It took place in Boston and was about a poor, wild, mistreated girl named Gertrude who was taken in and adopted by a very kind old man, a lamplighter by trade. I was promptly cheered to find myself in Gertrude's city. However, there were no streetlamps around, and in those rumbling underpasses it was hard to find a trace of the serene and spacious images I had constructed around the name of Boston in my distant childhood. Nonetheless the memory of *The Lamplighter* stayed with me the whole time I was in Boston, and in the end, after close scrutiny I found that the city was not so unlike the one I had unearthed from the ashes of my childhood fantasies. What I recalled about Gertrude was that in her most impoverished state she used to eat garbage. So I carefully examined the huge cans of garbage stationed in front of the houses on the Boston streets. In the morning my son explained to me that there were two cans for garbage, one for *organic* and the other for *inorganic.* Therefore, whenever I threw something out I had to stop to consider whether it went in the *organic* can or the *inorganic* can. Later when I was back in Italy I would still ponder over *organic* and *inorganic* even while I was throwing everything into one pail as we do here.

But to return to the evening of my arrival: my son and his wife immediately began discussing the long car trip through the Rocky Mountains that they were preparing to take with the baby. I had been aware of this plan for some time but in that violent thunderstorm the idea seemed crazy, and I said the baby would suffer from the cold. They pointed out that it was now May and the trip would take place in summer, so that the risk, if anything, was the sweltering heat. In any case, they added, they had shown the pediatrician their map and itinerary and he had given his approval. This pediatrician had his patients call him "Jerry." To arrange an appointment, he would send a postcard inscribed: "Jerry will be delighted to see Simone on Thursday at three o'clock." All the same, if Simone had had a fever of a hundred and four, Jerry would not have moved a millimeter, because he didn't make house calls. This was the rule and no pediatrician in America ever violated it. On the subject of Jerry, I also learned that he found Simone in good health but a bit overweight. Jerry liked babies to be thin. I found America to be a land of thin babies indeed. Moreover, the children didn't seem dressed warmly enough, and their hands were blue with cold because they didn't wear gloves.

When I first laid eyes on him, the evening of my arrival, Simone was wide awake in his crib, dressed in white cotton overalls and playing with a flat, plastic ginger cat. He was completely bald and had ironic black eyes, very keen and penetrating. If you looked quite carefully, you could make out a very fine blonde down on his bald head. His eyes were narrow and slanted toward his temples. He looked to me like Genghis Khan.

After several stormy days, a torrid summer suddenly broke out. At that point I said that it was dangerous to travel in such heat. I would have given anything to take the baby home with me to Italy, to the country, under shady, leafy trees. But his parents were adamant. They thought he would have more fun in the Rocky Mountains. I retorted that a baby of a few months couldn't tell the difference between the Rocky Mountains and a rabbit hutch. Sermons, complaints, and scoldings were my basic modes of expression during my stay in America. Mostly I couldn't relax, knowing that for three months this fragile, helpless creature would have no home. As a matter of fact my son and his wife had sublet their house until the month of October. Simone would be sleeping in the car, or in motels, or in a tent, a tent that had already been bought and that my son used to practice setting up on a friend's lawn. Until the beginning of October, Simone wouldn't have a roof over his head. Still, they told me, he would always have his own bed. This bed could actually be taken apart and folded up very small, then set up inside the car. Numerous tests of this procedure had also been made. I don't know if it was my son's lack of skill, but the process of setting up the bed in the car was extremely slow, and no less laborious than setting up the tent on the lawn.

I witnessed these preparations for the trip with mounting fear. Every day my son and his wife would come home with objects intended for the trip, huge plastic bottles for water and powders to prevent scorpion bites. They also bought an enormous plastic bag and tossed all the baby's toys in it. I remarked that this was a needless encumbrance, but they had read in Dr. Spock that a baby had to travel accompanied by all his toys. Since they couldn't always be consulting Jerry, they frequently sought answers and support in Dr. Spock.

Unaware of the threat of the Rocky Mountains, the baby lived in the house as if it had been his since the dawn of time. He stayed in his carriage on the wooden porch in front of the house, shaking his ginger cat and perusing the world with his Genghis Khan eyes. He was a beautiful, strong, plump baby, evidently too plump for Jerry's taste, and he gleefully gulped down bottles of milk but struggled fiercely against any other kind of food. I suggested giving him the renowned vegetable broth. In Italy babies are weaned on vegetable broth. But my son and his wife expressed great scorn for vegetable broth. And even I realized it was pointless to get the baby used to vegetable broth, which had to be boiled for hours and couldn't possibly be prepared while traveling by car.

Back home in Italy I was anxious all summer, notwithstanding the postcards and reassuring photos that arrived from the Rocky

Mountains showing the baby, naked and suntanned, sitting on his parents' shoulders. At the end of the summer, after they had returned home, I received a letter from my son telling me about the trip and relating, among other things, how one night bears had turned up at their campsite, probably attracted by the smell of syrup from a bottle that had broken on the roof of their car. Huddled in the tent with the baby in their arms, they had peered out at the bears rummaging around the car and raging over an ice chest. These were no cute little teddy bears but huge, heavy, menacing animals; to drive them away they had to bang pot covers together. At daybreak they had gone to the tourist office and asked them to recommend a campsite where bears never set foot.

Even though the incident was long over, this terrifying news upset me, and I wrote letters lecturing and scolding them. They returned to Italy after one more winter and a summer in which they took yet another trip, this time to the "deep South," a place I knew to be hot and perilous. I greeted the baby with the feeling that he had survived dangerous voyages. He was walking and talking now. He had very soft, fine blond hair on his long, delicate head. He had a few obsessions. He wouldn't touch fresh fruit and insisted on pear nectar in a bottle. He wouldn't wear wool sweaters because they had "hairs." The only garment he would consent to put on in the cold was a faded old windbreaker. I thought his aversion to "hairs" might derive from an aversion to or fear of those bears he had seen. But maybe that was a foolish inference on my part, since he'd been too young at the time to be afraid. Little by little we persuaded him that the "hairs" of the sweater would go away if he rubbed them hard on his sleeve. Still, the windbreaker remained his favorite garment.

One afternoon he was coming over to my house and I watched for him at the window. I spied him crossing the street with his father. He was walking along with a serious air, holding his father's hand yet absorbed in himself as if he were alone, carrying a nylon bag where he kept his windbreaker. His sister had just been born, which might have accounted for his seriousness. In his pace, his long, austere, delicate head, his dark and deeply knowing gaze, I suddenly perceived something Jewish that I had never seen before. He looked like a little immigrant. When he used to sit on the porch in Boston, he seemed to reign supreme over the world around him. He looked like Genghis Khan. Now he wasn't Genghis Khan anymore; the world had shown itself to be changeable and unstable, and he seemed to have been struck by a precocious awareness of the menacing, unreliable nature of things, of how a human being must learn to be self-sufficient. He seemed to know there was nothing he could call his own except that faded nylon bag containing four little plastic figures, two chewed pencils and a faded windbreaker. Little wandering Jew, crossing the street with his bag in his hand.

April, 1970

portrait of a writer

When the writer was young, she felt guilty about writing. She didn't know why. Writing was what she had wanted and intended to do from earliest childhood. And yet she felt guilty. She thought, in her confusion, that she ought to be studying and improving her mind, in order to write more serious things. She didn't study, but spent her time thinking she ought to be studying. The hours she spent writing felt like stolen hours.

Whenever she wrote, she felt she ought to be hurrying along to the end. Often in the past she hadn't finished what she began, and so finishing was her essential goal. Maybe then she would get over her sense of guilt. She was like a boy stealing grapes: in his whirlwind flight, troubling thoughts assail him; his head feels enveloped by a cloud of wasps. He has to bring his grapes to unknown people, remote, mysterious people he imagines as utterly different from himself and everyone around him. He's afraid of them. He's also afraid that avalanches and earthquakes will bar his path; he's afraid that when he gets there he'll find everyone vanished, the earth under their feet blown to bits.

She gave up writing, spent long years not writing at all. She got lost and forgot the paths that led to writing. Her hands were rusty, her thoughts muddled. Occasionally, amid her muddled thoughts, she would remember how she once used to write, and she felt she had betrayed her early goals. Then she would tell herself it was her duty to write again. And that stern resolution cast a sense of guilt over her life, which was now otherwise occupied. She often thinks she has found a way to feel guilty her entire life, for contrary reasons.

Old now, she writes very slowly. She stops a dozen times to do and undo. She has developed an extraordinary patience. Every so often she thinks that before she dies she must dredge up everything inside her. Yet the idea fails to rouse her. At times she thinks she has nothing left to dredge up, or has only very complex, tangled, contorted things. She has never enjoyed plunging into complexities. Now, however, her mind can get tangled in bizarre knots. Slowly, she tries to extricate herself. This slowness and patience are new and disagreeable—it would be far better to run like a thief.

She no longer feels she must offer her writing to remote, mysterious people. What she writes is meant for three or four people she sees often. In spells of depression, she imagines these three or four people understand nothing, and she asks fate to send her new people, or to give the old ones back their former insight. Even as she asks, she recalls that fate does not usually heed her requests.

She no longer fears earthquakes. She has gotten used to writing in harsh, inhospitable circumstances, oppressed by crushing misery, like someone who has learned to breathe under the weight of a heap of rubble.

In her youth she was blessed with imagination. Not much, but she did have a little. It worried her to have so little. Considering that since childhood she had resolved and expected to be a writer, a novelist, she found it quite odd to have so little imagination. She also seemed to lack the power of observation. She would seize on a number of tiny details from the world around her and keep them scrupulously in mind, but she perceived the whole as shrouded in a vaporous mist. She was very absentminded. Now and then she wondered what her characteristics as a writer were, and could find none. Sometimes she thought she wrote simply because she had decided to do so back in the distant past. Deep inside her was a dark whirling turmoil, like a subterranean river, and she felt her writing ought to spring from those waters. But she could not draw it to the surface.

Her imagination was neither daring nor lavish. It was an arid, grudging, frail imagination. She regarded it as a frail, delicate, precious possession: she was pulling a few sad, languishing flowers out of barren soil, while she would have liked a vast landscape of meadows and woods. So she felt impoverished. She must use her resources frugally. She was cautious, impetuous, and frugal all at once—impetuous especially because she felt that if she slackened, even her will might fail her.

Her frugality was actually more a form of avarice. She made up a few things and told them in swift, dry words. Since she wanted to love what she was writing, she gave her avarice the name of restraint. She was strongly determined to disregard her own weaknesses, or else to transform them into something noble, appealing, and praiseworthy.

But there were times when she was honest with herself. She admitted she didn't like her avarice. She felt she was prodigal by nature. She would have liked to write streams of whirling, tumultuous pages that were limpid and faultless as well. Instead her pages possessed a clarity that was swift, orderly, neat, and miserly. This clarity was deceptive, for in truth she saw the world around her as veiled in mist. Thus besides being a miser she was also a liar. Her avarice arose from the fear of revealing her barren, misty wasteland of a world. Through the stingy little crack opening onto that world, she would grasp and number its arid flowers. And all this in great haste, because of her sense of guilt. She felt like a thief, a stingy, nervous, calculating thief. In lucid moments, she found herself despicable.

Yet she lulled herself with the idea that later on, in the future, she would suddenly be endowed with great powers of invention and observation. She would have a green, boundless imagination, a wild expanse of woods. She would also enjoy a vast harvest of ideas. And then she would be assiduous and generous in bestowing her wealth.

Now her future is just a cracked, rutted stretch of road where no grass grows. Her imagination has disappeared. She no longer feels guilty; she's in no hurry. She has grown patient, and spends her time doing and undoing. She feels self-contempt rather than guilt—merely contempt, her patience being so disagreeable. Along with her imagination, her avarice has disappeared too: she has become generous and would give away all she has, only at times she suspects there is nothing left to give.

In her youth she was deeply envious of the books she had already written. She would study them, pore over them to figure out how she had managed to write them. Then she realized that any such quest was useless. She wasn't learning anything from her own books: staring at them was like staring at a blank wall.

She couldn't seem to maintain calm relationships with her books. Either she was too fond of them, or they made her sick. She never tired of reading them over and over, yearning to love them at any cost. She thought about them too much and too often. She thought they were written with admirable speed and restraint. What she now considers their basic flaw, their poverty of imagination and their short, nervous breath, used to seem beautiful and fill her with pride. Nonetheless, if anyone so much as ventured a critical word, she would suddenly detest those books and mentally rip them to shreds. Then for years they would inspire loathing, to the point of her never opening the cabinet where she had hidden them away. Now, on occasion these books come to mind; she may go to the cabinet, pick them up and leaf through them for a moment. She feels no envy, no loathing, only a slight disgust. Mostly they remind her of the periods when she wrote them, and how the places she invented mingled with fragments of the real places she was living in at the time—when she still had the imagination to invent and to mingle—places scattered through her memory and forming a geography where she alone can find her way about. She remembers how sad and lost she felt when she was finished and had to leave those places, like someone who has to leave a town whose every house and every alley is familiar, knowing for certain that he can never return; and recalling the great fury and speed of her writing back then, she wonders now what was her hurry, why she didn't stay a little longer in those places invented with such avarice yet such precision.

There are words and expressions in her books which over the years she has come to hate. Yet it never occurs to her to get rid of them and rewrite them. Many people have already read those words; destroying them would be futile. And besides, she would be loath to touch a word in those books; their words and phrases seem frozen, written in stone. After all this time she still doesn't have a calm relationship with her books. So she slams them shut and puts them away, hoping others will love them, seeing that she herself, in the end, no longer does. What she feels for her books is a sort of vain tolerance that coexists, even blends, with disgust. And yet the tolerance and the disgust both seem directed not so much at the books but rather at what she herself was when she wrote them.

With all that, she sometimes thinks that in not caring for her books, in refusing to rewrite the parts that offend her, there is something unlovely, a weary renunciation of ever being, in her own eyes, the limpid, flawless writer she had hoped to become.

She has no more will to invent. She doesn't know whether it's because she is tired and her imagination is dead—always scanty, frail and sick, now it is dead—or because she understands that she wasn't meant to invent but to tell what really happened, what she learned through others or on her own.

She doesn't know if she should weep for the death of her imagination as a loss or welcome it as a liberation.

In the past she did use some elements of her real life, but she constructed her inventions around them, mixing the two, so that those few elements became unrecognizable to herself as well as to others. That process of mixing and kneading was so swift that almost immediately she would forget she had done it, though all the while she would be anxiously muttering her calculations and weighing every ingredient on her meticulous, secret scales. She didn't feel like a thief but a cook, or better still, a pharmacist. At last she would have before her something in which the real had undergone a total and absolute metamorphosis.

Her spirit can no longer perform such a metamorphosis, or else refuses to perform it. Now when she wants to dredge up some fragment of her real life, knead it and manipulate it as she once did, each fragment seems to drag its whole context along with it. Her tiny scales have been knocked down and swept away. She no longer feels like a pharmacist or a cook. She doesn't even feel like a thief—she has no urge to run away. Anyhow, she wouldn't know where to run. She feels like herself. She's not a miser anymore—she couldn't possibly measure out the truth. And she needs to be slow and patient because what is before her is truth, sketching arabesques that are hard to decipher. Yet to decipher them is essential. Her mind can get tangled up in them and it's difficult to extricate herself since her reason is quite hesitant and confused. Also, every so often the fear strikes her that these arabesques may have meaning only for her. She's always hated the notion of writing only for herself. Even at her most miserly she couldn't bear that notion. The three or four people she usually writes for express contradictory opinions and she can't tell who's right or wrong, nor can she see anyone coming along to take their place. There are times when she's oppressed by the thought that maybe she is writing now simply to decipher herself, which seems a completely useless effort. She doesn't feel guilty, since she doesn't think she is capable of doing anything more useful. She has no plans or wishes to do anything else. She feels bound to this until death.

The truth brings home memories that make her suffer. Yes, she's used to writing while weighed down by a heap of rubble, but she is afraid that touching so many memories may scorch her hands and eyes. She's also afraid her memories may hurt others in her life, whom she loves. Compared to telling the truth, inventing was like playing with a litter of kittens. Telling the truth is like moving through a pack of tigers. She reminds herself that to a writer everything is permitted so long as she writes—even freeing tigers and taking them out for a stroll. But in fact she doesn't believe writers have any special rights, any more than others do. So she faces a problem she cannot resolve. She doesn't want to be a shepherd of tigers.

She thinks she has been on the wrong track from the very first moment she sat down to write as a child. She should have loved invention then as she loves truth now. But her love was small and cold. And in return, invention gave her only miserly, frozen images.

Now she asks that truth bring her what invention never gave. She realizes she is asking the impossible. As soon as she tries to tell the truth, she gets lost contemplating its violence and immensity.

She thinks she has done nothing but pile error upon error. How stupid she has been. She has also posed a great many stupid questions. She has asked whether writing, for her, was a duty or a pleasure. Stupid. It was neither. At the best of times it was, and is, her way of inhabiting the earth.

October, 1970

film

I saw at an art cinema a film written by Beckett and performed by Buster Keaton. It was called *Film*. It lasts less than half an hour and has no words. A man, in a room, puts an end to his life. We don't see him die or kill himself, but it is clear that after these few moments it will be all over for him.

In the room are a bed, a blanket, a mirror, a large rocking chair, a cat and a dog in a basket, a fish in a tank, a parrot in a cage. Despite the furniture and animals, the room feels stripped and empty. The moment when the man placed the bed and the mirror, the basket, the tank and the cage there seems far, far away, lost in a time beyond memory.

With anxious, terrified movements, as if pursued by invisible tormentors, the man covers the mirror with a cloth, puts the dog and cat outside, shuts the door again, covers the tank and the cage. Then he sits on the rocker in the middle of the room and rocks. From time to time he takes his pulse, with the apprehensive solicitude for himself, for his own heartbeat, of a man who has no one else on earth, with the fear of death of a man who desires nothing more except death.

He takes some photographs out of a leather briefcase and studies them. They are ancient pictures of a person he once was. Childhood, his mother's face, school holidays, athletic competi-

[139]

tions, marriage, a woman, a child. Images of a life with breathing space, infused with a mild, warm affection. A life remote from that room and its desolate furnishings. For a moment, his thumb strokes the picture of the child. One by one, he tears all the photographs in half. He tears them in half one by one, with no hesitation and no anxiety now, but carefully, painstakingly. He lets them fall to the floor.

Until now we have not seen his face, just his hands, his shoulders, his scarf, the cracks in the wall, the folds of the blanket. At last we see his face: ravaged, hollowed out, a black patch over one eye. Only for an instant, then he quickly hides this face with his ravaged hands. A single, final gesture of compassion for himself; a single, final attempt to hide his own image, to sink beyond reason and memory; a single, final entreaty to darkness, nothingness and death.

This swift, silent tale could be enacted only by Buster Keaton. It is impossible to imagine any other person in that role. He is not acting: he *is* that man. I don't know much about Buster Keaton's life, only what may be common knowledge. He died some years ago, alone and penniless. His final days were probably very similar to those of the man in the room.

He suffered a cruel fate. He was a hugely famous comic actor in the era of silent films; with the advent of sound, he was no longer sought out and quickly forgotten. It was inconceivable in any case that words should ever escape his lips. His gaunt, parched face with its sealed lips, unfit for smiling, its rigid and tense jaws, was the very mask of silence. He was a great actor, a great comic actor. The comedy came from his deft movements, his silence, and his fixedness.

His photos would occasionally appear in the newspapers: a face on which time and obscurity had carved shadows and furrows. A face covered with a dense network of wrinkles, like a map. The lips always sealed up tight. He must have sealed himself in his silence as in a tomb, though still alive. He had just a few brief minor roles. He was the pianist in *Limelight*. *Film* must have been one of his last films if not the last, and I don't think it had any distribution.

Chaplin had a very different fate. I believe they were friends in their youth. Chaplin possessed in abundance all that Keaton after a time no longer had. Once past the harshness of his early years as a poor orphan, Chaplin had glory, money, and honor and would have them for the rest of his life. His glory has long been indestructible.

He was, no doubt, the greater actor. The world of his childhood, the dismal back alleys of the poor, very quickly became a distant memory, and for many years he drew his inspiration from that grim memory. He invented the immortal character we know so well, the darting, limping figure with the black curls framing a pale face, the meek, luminous smile. He too was speechless. He too knew well enough the pathetic inadequacy of human speech.

In old age Chaplin transformed himself into a person in some ways the exact opposite of that limping, wandering vagabond. He became a florid, white-haired old man, an optimist and millionaire. He lives in a villa in Switzerland with a pack of children. If by chance the long-gone limping vagabond and this shrewd, florid old gentleman were to meet, they would have nothing to say to each other. The aged Chaplin wrote and gave speeches, even published a memoir.

When we come across that former figure whom we love on the screen, we have to separate him from what we know of the person who created him, and then turned into someone so different. We have to dispel all memory of the thoughts expressed in his book, his cheery affirmations, his quite disingenuous vanity, the sturdy, robust person whose every instinct of flight has totally vanished. Whose every instinct of freedom has vanished too.

In old age Chaplin made a number of awful films. They did very well. The idea of having made awful films surely never even occurred to him, as he had grown too self-congratulatory by that time to address himself with any honesty. That in itself would be of no importance, however; his awful films cannot detract from his genius. When we see on the screen the immortal character he once created, we don't think of his final awful films. We think rather of who he is now, on the far shore from what he once was.

We cannot reproach him for having become a rich, shrewd old man. A person can be quite rich and quite shrewd, yet manage somehow to remain a free spirit. It is difficult, I imagine, but not impossible. More likely what is so depressing about him today is actually his optimism. The things he thinks and writes. The pathetic, hollow optimism of an octogenarian for whom everything turned out just fine.

Buster Keaton, as far as I know, left no memoirs. The silence within him and the silence surrounding him must have been immense. Old age vented its fury on him, laying waste his body and his parched, bare, defenseless face. And yet he remained himself, sealed in his silence, loyal to the infinite despair that could only be speechless, human speech being so pathetically inadequate, forever loyal to the infinite freedom of never uttering a single word.

May, 1970

universal compassion

I believe the worst of our present misfortunes is our great difficulty, in the face of whatever event, in distinguishing the victims
from the oppressors. No matter what transpires, whether public
or private, our intellectual response is to avidly pursue the root
causes and seek out the probable guilty parties. But before long
we stop short in bewilderment: the causes appear numberless,
the reality too tortuous and complex for human judgment. We
have come to recognize that no event, public or private, can be
considered or judged in isolation, for the more deeply we probe,
the more we find infinitely ramifying events that preceded it, all
the way back to its source. In such a subterranean labyrinth,
tracking down the guilty and the innocent seems a hopeless
quest. The truth darts from place to place, slipping and sliding
in the dark like a fish or a mouse.

We have seen firsthand, in matters both private and public,
how those whom we loved and sympathized with as victims can
change overnight, taking on the odious guises of cruelty and
persecution. And yet we can't help regarding them as the victims
they once were. We don't know whether to understand and pity
them as victims, as before, or to judge them solely in this new
guise. Moreover, it seems dreadful, incomprehensible, that those

who have been victimized can use violence on their fellow men and fail to see in them their own likeness, as of only yesterday.

If we probe still more deeply, we come to realize there is no human being who has not suffered injustice, no human circumstances that do not merit understanding. But with such universal understanding, no one remains to be judged or condemned. Individual responsibility and moral judgment are apparently doomed to vanish from the face of the earth.

The fact remains that those of us who are older can vividly recall a not-too-distant past when taking one side or the other and distinguishing justice from injustice was a matter of the utmost simplicity. Truth's likeness, back then, was clear, unmistakable, and unshakeable; it was close at hand—we always knew where to find it. We could never have imagined that one day it might seem hidden and elusive. Not only were events simple to judge, presenting themselves in primary colors, with truth's limpid, radiant image shining above them; not only was our conception of reality far less vast and cluttered, so that we could act in good faith on our indignation or our approval. We also had no inkling that innocence and guilt are so often mingled, tangled in such tight knots that human beings, with their crude and inadequate yardsticks and their faulty senses, are quite unable to unravel them. We had no inkling yet that human beings are weak and without the resources to grasp the complexity of world events. This awareness of our inability to distinguish the truth and pursue it through its endless implications, explanations, and ramifications is a source of profound misery.

When confronted with some specific act that would inevitably be labeled cruel or unjust, we tell ourselves, or we are told, that even more unjust, more cruel, and more bloody acts are taking place in other parts of the world. Thus the sense of outrage is always deferred or projected elsewhere. When we think we can pin the evil and guilt on a specific person, on whom we long to vent our legitimate loathing, we tell ourselves, or we are told, that behind that person stand institutions, a maze of powerful vested interests, and that if we consider his position carefully, he too is ultimately no more than a defenseless and guiltless victim. We've also learned, or have been told, that our outrage at or endorsement of individuals is of no importance; the important thing is not to be outraged or supportive but rather to examine the causes and origins of every event. We think, or we are told, that it is foolish to use our customary yardstick of good and evil. We ourselves find it crude, inadequate, and obsolete. Using it feels like using a spade, while our hands and minds have grown used to compasses and calculators. We're ashamed to use such a crude domestic tool. And yet, however much we deride its crudeness, we still believe this kind of tool to be indispensable. Without it, the world becomes utterly indecipherable. True, it may be an inadequate yardstick for the huge and cluttered range of events we face at present; and true, we no longer know how to use it, with our hands grown so weak and unreliable. Perhaps there is some secret way to make such an instrument more subtle, more articulated, more sensitive, to transform it so it might keep pace with our understanding. But we don't know this secret way; we are nowhere near knowing it. And so the tool for judging good and evil drops from our hands like a spade, and all we can do is lament its crudeness and deficiencies.

Whether we are witnesses or protagonists, our instinctive reaction to whatever happens, private or public, is anger or approval. Weighed down by love and hate, we are forever seeking a place to unload them. But we cannot find the right place or the right person, since we tell ourselves, or we are told, that individual responsibilities in such complex matters are of minimal importance; and so we carry around this terribly heavy burden of love and hate, not knowing what to do with it, until it rots and withers in our arms, then drops to our feet. And all the while we gaze fixedly at reality, our eyes glazed with weariness and universal commiseration.

To grant any value to our moral judgment is too daunting; to use it feels too shameful; all we have at our disposal today is a vast compassion for ourselves and the world at large. With universal compassion, surely we can't go wrong. It is the one feeling we can give ourselves up to without fear of error. Such a flood of pity, in ourselves and others, may seem bizarre, given that our world and its vicissitudes are consummately cruel and pitiless, offering not the faintest glimpse of the profound pity that imbues us. Then again, our compassion is informed neither by intelligence nor by any real will to improve the world or ourselves. It is merely the result of fatigue and confusion, like a nervous outburst of tears that leaves us prostrate but unchanged. In any case, tears cannot lead us astray, for without a doubt, the world we find ourselves in has earned them.

In this kind of world, the winners' faces can very readily turn loathsome. Victory swiftly takes on gigantic proportions—monstrous, unreal, cut loose from the human community. A world made up of the weak and the wretched hates the advent of winners, knowing that all too soon they will take on inhuman ways and unreal, dismal, lugubrious garb. Therefore even if we don't know which side to support, we feel somehow drawn to the side of the losers. That is all we can do, in our desperate, confused quest for someone we can love without fear of error. Ours is not so much a moral choice but rather a yielding to an instinct of affinity. We cannot even imagine a happy world where the winners would not be hateful. Only in the losers can we recognize any kindred spirits—for if we call them ill-fated, battered victims, for the time being, at least, we feel sure we cannot go wrong.

October, 1970

vita immaginaria (*Fantasy Life*) was published by Mondadori in 1974, when the author was 58. The essays show the accumulated wisdom of maturity, but even more, they show its impatience and defiant freedom. Ginzburg never hesitated to criticize, but here, as in "No Fairies, No Wizards," or the pieces about the discordant chaos of contemporary Rome, she does so with positive relish. And in "Fantasy Life" she probes her intimate life—the life of the imagination—more deeply than ever before. The results are startlingly frank and unsettling. Yet her acceptance of her own bitter experience and decline is so unstintingly felt and rendered that it amounts to an affirmation of the darkest kind: that is the note Ginzburg strikes perpetually, and nowhere more purely than here.

such is rome

Though it seems to do its utmost to be as ugly as possible, I still find Rome, the city I live in, very beautiful. Besides finding it so beautiful, I love it dearly and wouldn't leave it for anything in the world. Nevertheless, it has become quite difficult both to love it and to live in it, since these days it is a jungle of automobiles. If ever there was a city made for walking, it's this one; the cars seem to have invaded it by stealth, like an attack of blight. I cannot understand who wanted them, since everyone curses them. They overrun the city like a river at flood tide, they appear to have erupted from the bowels of the earth, and every so often they fill the city with a long, exasperated, mocking shriek that sounds at once like a jeer and a cry for help.

The cities we choose to make our own, as adults, are a composite of the image we had of them in childhood, before we ever saw them; the image they presented when we saw them for the first time; the yearning we've felt when far away; and finally, our indifference or anger as we walk through them after long years of residence. The feelings they inspire in us after so many years are no different from the feelings inspired by people, when a prolonged and daily habit of living together has streaked our love with intolerance and anger. At some point we become aware that the intolerance and anger, grown over the love like lichen, have not worn it down but rather made it stronger, deeper, and inextinguishable. Then we try to call up distant images of these people or these places at our first encounter, when we didn't yet know whether it was to be a minor, fleeting encounter or something essential and enduring.

We often tend to compare the cities we chose as adults with those where we spent our childhood. Often we congratulate ourselves for having pulled up our early roots and set down new roots and habits elsewhere. And, strange to say, having grown old now, we maintain this peculiar pride in having sunk roots and habits far from our childhood landscapes. Why we should feel such pride is a mystery, since one doesn't deserve any special credit, in the scheme of things, for having left one's city of origin. And yet, till our dying day, the inexplicable banner of our pride flutters over the cities we chose as adults.

In the past, when I had spent brief periods in Rome or when I recalled it longingly from far away, I used to enumerate the reasons why I loved it. I thought that I loved its strange air of seeming small while it was enormous. At night in Rome, one had the feeling of ambling down village lanes. What made it resemble a village might have been the cats or the silence or the rich peace of certain vast, deserted piazzas, or the uncanny, pervasive sense of an invisible countryside, wooded and boundless, quite close by. How on earth the country could seem so close by, in those stony surroundings, that we could feel, amid the darkness, the rustling expanse of fields and trees, I cannot say. We could sit down on a staircase, gaze at the cats, the grass, the moon, the fountains and the ruins, and enjoy a strange and solemn pastoral silence. We could think it was summer when in fact it was winter. I found the seasons in this city often jumbled, which felt extraordinary to one who grew up in Turin. I was used to Turin's interminable freezing winters, when fog and darkness would hold the city clamped and stiff in a stern, impenetrable slumber. It seemed Rome could never sink so totally into winter, for beyond the cold one could always be surprised by an unlikely whiff of indolence, of summer vacations. It seemed a place where something unpredictable was always happening. When it rained and the entire city was like one enormous puddle, there might appear in the midst of the rain, from I don't know where, a sudden warmth and glimmer of spring. A sky heavy with swollen yellow clouds might suddenly be lit by a fiery twilight color. All these reasons were why I thought I loved it. Still, it is true that during my first few years in Rome I pined with homesickness for Turin and its endless winters. Even as I walked through Rome or leaned against its balustrades thinking how warm and mild the stone here always felt, I had a wrenching nostalgia for Turin and specifically for one street in Turin, and that was Via Nizza. Why I yearned for Via Nizza I don't know. It was a street in my old neighborhood, but not the street where I grew up. And yet I would have given anything at all to be on Via Nizza, walking among its very tall buildings sealed with ice, breathing in its fog, its winter and melancholy.

Indeed I think my early love for Rome was mingled with that nostalgia for Turin, my native city, from which, at that time, the war kept me. Our feelings for cities, like our feelings for people, are always rather confused, with all sorts of things mixed in. What is clear is that we don't love cities, or love people, for any reasons that can be enumerated. In the Rome of today I don't see the slightest trace of the reasons for which I once claimed to love it. It's no longer possible to look at the sky here, or to be aware of the seasons. It's not even possible to exchange an affectionate word or glance with the city anymore. Cars overrun its sidewalks. It is stricken by cars as by some malignant disease. Nothing, nowadays, feels as distant and remote as the country-

side. The cats and the ruins remain, but it never occurs to anyone to look at them—you'd have to seek them out behind the
cars. And at night Rome definitely doesn't feel like a village. But
it doesn't feel like a great, restless city either, not by night or by
day; the fact is that it doesn't feel like anything. It's as if it no
longer knows what to be. The cars do thin out at night, but the
silence in the streets now is never tranquil and profound. It is a
silence without peace, an expectant silence, prostrate with exhaustion. It is a silence still vibrating with the echo of that lacerating, querulous shriek, the shriek of cars tied up in traffic, and
the whole city waits for that shriek to start all over again very
soon, with its harrowing, mocking appeal for help. Around the
edges of the city, houses keep springing up that bear no resemblance to it nor to each other, all of them dreadful but each one
dreadful in its own individual way, houses that appear leprous
and decrepit from the moment they are built. They don't know
what to be either—city houses or country houses—yet they seem
to seek a connection with the city's center. The only connection
they manage to achieve, though, is that they too writhe in the
stranglehold of the cars. Years ago, an outcropping of new
houses had already sprouted up on the edges, a tangled, de-
formed, fragile vegetation, but the city, in its supreme and oblivious indifference, seemed able to shelter and sustain every
species of deformity. Now its indifference, apparently doomed
to last forever, has given rise to a vague weariness, a hidden baf-
flement and sadness, in a city which was never weary or baffled
or sad. It is the sadness of having lost its essential nature and
being unable to assume another.

This is the Rome of today, which I no longer like, which no
one seems to like, and yet we all love it, for the truth is that cities,
like people, are loved for no reason at all or for a tangle of reasons, different for everyone. In Rome during the war, I lived in

hiding in a convent on Via Nomentana, sharing a room with an
old Jewish woman from Vienna whom I made friends with. She
was very kind, and when I went out she would mind my infant
daughter. I had a small electric stove, and now and then this little old lady would ask if she could use it. Although I had told her
many times that she could use it whenever she liked, still she
would announce every time she was about to use it. On cold afternoons, she would get up from the bed and say, "My dear Signora, I make myself the tea." One might well ask how in the
world this little old woman in exile, whom I haven't seen since
and who must be long dead, enters into my feelings for the city.
But for me, Via Nomentana and the dark corridor of the convent and its high windows grazed by trees are inseparable from
the memory of that very tiny old woman sitting on the bed in a
brown shawl, and I think I began to love Rome while seeking
some kind of maternal protection in that little old woman, who
in turn wanted my protection along with my stove. So that now,
when I go down Via Nomentana, buried in cars and unrecognizable, I remember how beloved that street is to me; I recover
the keys to my affection by murmuring those long-lost words,
"My dear Signora, I make myself the tea."

December, 1970

no fairies, no wizards

The publisher Giulio Einaudi is bringing out a new series of children's books called "Tantibambini," edited by Bruno Munari. Four books are already available. I received them. They were very nice, I thought. Inexpensive. Pleasing to the eye. Easy to handle. I thought the best illustrations were those accompanying a selection of Edward Lear's *Nonsense Verses*. There's also a book by Gianni Rodari, a story called *Mr. Cat's Business*. I read it quickly and found it quite charming. Gianni Rodari is one of Italy's very few writers of children's books. Children adore his books. I myself prefer his poetry to his prose, but children love his stories as well (at least the children I know). So far so good. And yet there was something bothering me and I wasn't sure what it was. Another book is called *Birdie Tic Tic*, by an author called Poi. I don't know who this Poi is. I read that one quickly too—it only takes a couple of minutes. It's about a little boy who's afraid of a wolf, but Birdie Tic Tic feeds the wolf, he gives him lots of onions, sardine heads and old shoes, the wolf isn't hungry anymore and becomes good, the boy isn't afraid anymore. A sweet story. At some point I realized that what was irritating me were the words that appeared on the back of every volume: "Simple stories and fairy tales—no witches and no fairies, no splendid castles or handsome princes or mysterious wizards—written for a new generation of free spirits, uninhibited, assertive, and fully aware of their own strength." Little by little I realized that I found these words not merely irritating but detestable. They struck me as hugely presumptuous. Had *Birdie Tic Tic* been presented casually, without any such pretensions, and had this series legitimately embraced children's books of every kind and genre, well then, fine, but if *Birdie Tic Tic* was being offered as heralding a pedagogical program and as the bible of the coming generations, in that case, I decided, *Birdie Tic Tic* was revolting.

In light of my irritation I reread *Birdie Tic Tic* and didn't find it at all sweet. The moral of *Birdie Tic Tic* is that by feeding wolves you render them harmless. This is not true. Whoever wrote it thought it would be a good idea to demystify a child's concept of a wolf. And yet wolves do exist. However much you appease their hunger, they are still wolves and they still eat people. Besides actual wolves, there are people who resemble wolves; the world is full of them. I don't see what benefit there is for children in thinking that wolves become tame if you feed them. Nor do I see any benefit in children's not fearing wolves. It's a mistake to think fear is something bad. Fear is something one must endure and learn to tolerate.

Furthermore, wolves do not eat onions. A wolf that eats onions and old shoes is no less remote from reality than a witch or a fairy. Therefore I would like to know why this collection has banished witches and fairies as obsolete and reactionary, fit only for older generations that quenched their thirst on fantasy and illusion, and has meanwhile spread the welcome mat for this onion-eating wolf.

In light of my irritation I reread all four books in the series and concluded that while each one in itself was fine, the prospect of others in the same vein was suffocating. Everything was predictable and foreordained. Children's books should be as full of adventure and surprise as a forest. These were more like wooden scaffoldings.

I can't work up any genuine irritation towards Bruno Munari, the editor of the series, since I don't know him. But Giulio Einaudi, the publisher, is a friend, and a very dear one. I can never be indifferent to anything he does or thinks. So all my irritation is really directed at him. Some years ago he published the most wonderful children's book ever written in our time: *Italian Folktales*, by Italo Calvino. This is a marvelous book, filled with fairies, magicians, splendid princes and magnificent castles. Also peasants and fishermen. Reading it, you breathe the free air of fantasy as well as the harsh, free air of reality. It contains no moral lessons other than those implicit ones that real life offers every day. It has no pedagogical intentions whatsoever. It is written in a limpid, linear, concrete prose, an exemplary prose that illustrates how one should write for children, prose without a single superfluous word. I challenge anyone to find a single superfluous word. I challenge anyone to find even a single affected word. Surely Calvino had no educational motive in mind, but in truth nothing is more educational than style when it is clear, swift, and concrete. The *Italian Folktales* are authentic fairy tales, generously created for the joy of his fellow readers, which is how children's fairy tales must be conceived and created— purely for pleasure. It is true that Calvino didn't make these stories up himself; he gathered them from Italian tradition and rewrote them, but by rewriting them in his swift, limpid prose he made them his own. Children of all ages were and still are enraptured by the *Italian Folktales*. The publisher, Giulio Einaudi, sold mountains of them. He hasn't forgotten, either, for he keeps them continuously in print. Did Giulio Einaudi realize that he had published an essential book in the field of children's literature? Does he know or doesn't he? If he knows, how could he ever come up with this latest phrase, "no fairies and no wizards"? It's like saying, "We're going to serve you an excellent cake made with no flour, no sugar, and no butter."

Instead, the publisher and editor of this series should have frankly stated: "Writing for children is extremely difficult these days. Few writers are up to the task. We are putting together the handful of successful examples. There are unfortunately no new stories with fairies and magicians. Sad but true. Calvino's *Italian Folktales* is a masterpiece, a miracle, but masterpieces and miracles are rare in the nature of things. So we'll do the best we can and you'll have to make do with what's available."

This might not be a very good advertising slogan. So what? If I were publishing or editing a series of children's books, I would have these words printed in big letters on every volume.

Among the countless reasons why writing for children is so difficult these days, certainly one is our current notion that everything is harmful to children. Imagination terrifies us because it is daring, unpredictable, and powerful. We possess little enough as it is, and what little we have we dole out sparingly and fastidiously. The top priority in writing or publishing children's books is barring the doors and windows. No sad stories because sadness is bad for children. No stories about poverty because they're tearjerkers. No tears. No emotion. No cruelty. No villains because children don't need to know about villainy. No good people because goodness is sentimental. No blood because it's too shocking. No magnificent castles because they're escapist. No fairies because they don't exist. Children are fragile, so we'll nourish them only on what has been scrubbed and disinfected. We'll teach them the facts of life, but first we'll sterilize those facts and filter out anything that gleams or glitters. We'll nourish them on sand, carefully strained and germfree. We'll nourish them on baking soda and talcum powder and blotting paper.

Some may object that children like baking soda. It may well be that they like it when they have nothing else. But the issue is not whether or not children like it. The issue is rather what this kind of diet will make of them.

In Calvino's *Italian Folktales*, which I can never tire of alluding to, there are severed heads, corpses, bandits, thieves, ogres, cruelty and horrors. All of this children relish, for genuine and beautiful fairy tales are in fact harmless. Their setting is the one place in the universe where there is no harm or danger, and that is the realm of the imagination. Whatever fear they may inspire is the imagination's healthy and liberating fear, a fear the spirit craves and reaches out to, as to a warming flame. Children hunger and thirst for the life of the imagination. Fairies and wizards exist in their fantasies, and the fact that they don't exist in reality is quite rightly irrelevant to them, since everything in the realm of the imagination is by its very nature invisible and intangible. In the realm of the imagination, even the most horrible images can bring joy. We all know that joy may include even fear and anguish. Suppressing fear and anguish means suppressing joy as well.

I should add that what I detest in the words "no fairies and no witches...for a new generation of free spirits, uninhibited, assertive, and fully aware of their own strength," is the rhetoric and optimism in regard to future generations. By all means let us hope that the coming generations are made up of free spirits. However, we really don't have any idea what they will be like. We don't even know for sure if it's good to grow up without inhibitions. One of these days we might discover that those very inhibitions people nowadays take such pride in having cast off—along with their individual struggles to overcome them or live with them—were the bread and salt of the spirit.

April, 1972

an invisible government

I 've always found it rather strange that after an election, nearly all the party newspapers proclaim victory even if they've been defeated. If I were a party leader, I would proclaim the truth in big red letters. If we had suffered a major defeat, the headline in my paper would read: "Major Defeat For Our Party." I can't see why every party newspaper instead finds it necessary to display exultant, triumphant headlines after each election. The few exceptions after the recent elections were remarkable indeed.

It will be pointed out that this is unimportant, since people read the voting returns and learn how things turned out in any case. It will also be pointed out that newspapers, whether partisan or nonpartisan, carry far more murky and lethal lies. That is true. The triumphant headlines have become a convention, like the conventional hellos and good-byes of a social call. People expect them and pay no attention. True enough. But if I were a party chief and my party had lost, I would go around shouting it from the rooftops. For in politics as elsewhere, the truth is salutary and invigorating.

It has been explained to me many times that the rules and procedures of politics are totally different from those of ordinary human life. It's been explained that political power operates by delicate, subtle mechanisms that are highly sensitive, and comprehensible maybe only to those who control them and can peer into their depths. The desire for truth, indeed any customary expectation of the human mind, has about as much weight on the machinery of political power as a swarm of gnats.

There are people who understand nothing of politics. I am one of them. There aren't many such people, in fact there may be very few, since almost everyone manages to master a handful of essential notions that permit them to understand the terms and structures of politics. Certain people, however, not only understand nothing of politics but are incapable of thinking politically. They are even less able to express themselves in political terms. I am one of those.

The people who do understand politics cannot begin to conceive of what we, the ones who understand nothing, are all about. So I want to explain, since after all, I know.

Thinking and expressing oneself politically means thinking and expressing oneself with a specific purpose in mind. Such a purpose might be aboveboard or corrupt; its ultimate goal might serve justice or oppression. Those who understand nothing of politics, on the other hand, think and express themselves without any goal whatsoever. It may be that their only goal is to explore and express their genuine thoughts. To the politically-minded, such a goal seems pointless. And at times it seems utterly pointless to those who understand nothing of politics too, which makes them despair. However, speaking their minds is the single thing in the world that they know how to do. At other times, they hope that what they say may strike a responsive chord in others. This is nothing like a specific goal, merely a stray hope.

When those who understand nothing about politics venture to speak of it, they either lapse into confusion and abstraction or talk nonsense. So it is more than likely that what I'm writing

here is a string of nonsense. Still, I must confess that despite understanding nothing of politics, I nonetheless often feel an over-
powering temptation to speak of it.

Beyond politics, there are countless other things about
which I know and understand nothing, such as economics, or
chemistry, or the natural sciences, or the exact sciences. But my
lack of understanding of those subjects doesn't disturb me. I get
along fine without them. They proceed far from my life and almost never cross my mind. Understanding nothing of politics,
on the contrary, feels like a serious disability. It pains and em-
barrasses me. People I've confided in tell me it's simply laziness
and resistance on my part. I am aware of being very lazy, and yet
I have the sense that my utter failure to understand politics is
not a question of laziness so much as a real disability.

When I was young, I thought that some time or other I would
read books in order to gain some understanding and background in politics. After a while I noted that whenever I opened
those books, my mind would dart away like a hare. And so I have
never read a single line of them. I also noted, after a while, that
all the novels and other books I had ever read were read without
any fixed purpose.

Even though I understand nothing of politics, political
events do occasionally arouse my hatred or indignation or approval and passion. But these events don't strike me as part of
any coherent, lucid, and harmonious pattern; they always seem
like fragments or splinters or bits of driftwood I'm clinging to
like someone left floundering in a river at flood tide.

One of the very few political ideas within my grasp, perhaps
the only one, I acquired when I was seven years old. It was explained to me what socialism was, that is, I was told it meant
equal distribution of goods and equal rights for all. It struck me
as something that had to be achieved right away. I found it

strange that it hadn't already been achieved. I remember the exact time and place when I heard these words, which were self-evident and crucial. To this day they still have the power to kindle a kind of flame in me. To this day I marvel that that state of affairs, namely, equal distribution of goods and equal rights, has not been achieved, and is apparently so complex and difficult to achieve.

When I have to vote, I follow emotional impulses; my inclinations are entirely of an emotional nature, as if I had to shake hands with a political party or kiss it on both cheeks. This is definitely not the proper way to vote. I know that. Each time, I'm given instructions, and each time, I cast them to the winds and instinctively follow only irrational affections and affinities. I find myself unable to vote for any party with resignation; I have to love the party I'm voting for. When I go to vote, that single rudimentary political idea that I possess, equal distribution of goods and equal rights for all people, flares up. I want to find out with absolute certainty who supports that, but since the explanations I get are conflicting and garbled, I end up voting blindly and emotionally.

People I know and trust have often told me that if equal rights and equal distribution of goods were attained, I would lose a part of my freedom, I wouldn't write anymore, and I would be terribly unhappy. This is because equal rights and equal distribution of goods don't fall like manna from heaven but require a number of strategic and terrifying protections. In fact I too think that if I couldn't write anymore I would be very unhappy and might throw myself under a train. But I also think that our personal happiness or unhappiness should not determine our political choices. What works quite well for us personally may not work at all well for others. We want a better world, but it could be that this better world has no place for us. And yet, it is conceivable to regard our own personal destiny with some detachment. I don't know if this kind of reasoning is political, that is, the kind of reasoning political people would accept. It is the reasoning of those who are desperate. I don't know if there is a place in politics for the desperate. I imagine not.

Then again, maybe governments never run smoothly. Some, at any rate, are overthrown. The government I myself would want would be totally bland, insubstantial, invisible, a government so airy and invisible that we could forget all about it, not even notice that it exists. Under such a government, everyone would live well, everyone would have his rightful place and role and his rightful share of benefits and freedom. Granted, a government of this kind doesn't exist in nature; nowhere are there any visible traces of it. In every existing government we find clamor, abuses of power, newspapers with triumphant, lying headlines, lies of every kind in public life. This being the case, someone like me, who understands nothing of politics, is compelled to think about politics in despair of ever understanding it, and is likewise compelled to envision something entirely different.

In truth, the airy, light, insubstantial and invisible government I conjure up might be a weak government, and in politics, weakness apparently has no chance at all of survival. It would be a weak government, because in politics strength is noisy, intrusive, huge, and bloodthirsty. It would be a government without money or weapons, founded solely on a few values that are precious to the spirit, such as justice, truth, and liberty. But the word "truth" is seldom used in politics, and the justification offered for its absence is the nature of those very delicate, fragile, and sensitive mechanisms at the core of political life, which demand the most specialized and highly refined precautions. As for liberty and justice, we are told that for the time being they must be protected by weapons, police, and prisons; we are told it is essential to protect them by force, and meanwhile we have this irrepressible craving for weakness.

We are told that in the distant future, maybe after centuries of weapons and prisons, all will be well at last; there will be enough space and liberty for everyone. At last, we'll no longer need to think in terms of nation-states, of masses of people and of governments, but only of our distinctive and solitary condition as human beings. But no one believes in the future anymore. Years ago, we could believe in it; the music of tomorrow, authentic and intoxicating, rang in our ears. Then all at once the future collapsed before our very eyes. So while we long for a better world, we can't project our longings to centuries from now. We don't have centuries to wait anymore, and even if we did, we have lost the will and the imagination to grasp what shape they might take. Right now we stubbornly love the present; we find ourselves lashed by bonds of love to a time that gives no sign of loving us in return.

June, 1972

summer

hate the summer. I hate the month of August up to the fifteenth, the Feast of the Assumption.* Once that's past, I feel like I'm emerging from a nightmare. Everything gradually improves. The autumn rains begin. I love autumn; in autumn I usually write something. In summer I very rarely manage to write.

I don't hate summer because of the heat. I don't notice the heat; it doesn't affect me in the least. I am reminded that it's hot only when others talk about it. To tell the truth, I have often tried to figure out why I hate the summer so much.

In childhood I liked summer; it was my favorite season. I delighted in the heat and the first cherries. Turin had lots of horse-drawn carriages back then, and in summer the coachmen would put net hoods over the horses' heads to keep the flies away. I used to say the horses were "wearing fairy hats," and I was overjoyed at the first sight of the horses in their "fairy hats."

Summer meant going away on vacation. Our enormous, ancient trunks with their rusty iron plates would appear in the hall, looking like dinosaurs. My mother panted and sighed as she packed them. Neither she nor my brothers liked going on

---

* Italian national holiday

vacation: they found it boring. I had a good time. We spent four months in the mountains, the place and the house determined by my father. In my mother's view, the houses were invariably uncomfortable and the places boring, with never a soul to say two words to. I participated in the packing rituals with enthusiasm, my joy only slightly dimmed by my mother's ill humor.

Once in the mountains, I pretended I had been born and raised there and would remain forever. I strove to erase all memories of our city house. I had no other children to play with, and I wandered through the fields alone, hunting for frogs and grasshoppers. I had no inkling of boredom then, or if I felt it at all, it was fleeting—I would sulk around the house for a while, only to be promptly scolded. For my father, boredom was always a crime, but especially so in the mountains. My mother, on the other hand, seemed to think only she and my brothers were entitled to be bored. I was too young to have any such right. My mother thought children should never sulk or loiter idly. She told me to wash my face and do my summer homework assignments. I paid no attention, well aware that doing summer assignments was one of the worst possible ways to combat boredom.

Anyway, I could shake off my boredom quite easily. Every afternoon might hold the promise of something extraordinary. I could go to the fields and find a huge toad. There were squirrels in the woods, and I never gave up the hope of catching one and bringing it home. Or I might try writing a novel or baking a cake or might even, out of the blue, make some great scientific discovery. My parents and my brothers would be amazed. I was always longing to amaze them, because I found it hard to get their attention. No matter what I did, no matter how amazing, they were never amazed.

The day we left the mountains was almost more wonderful, even, than the day we arrived. The excitement of leaving, first boarding a bus and then a train, was enhanced by the subtle, delectable sadness of bidding farewell to summer—sadness, for me, being something so slight and unaccustomed back then that it lent charm to happiness. Sadly, I took leave of those places I might never see again. My father said that next year we would go someplace else, someplace cheaper. In addition, at the end of every vacation and over the course of the winter, my father would say that we wouldn't be taking any more vacations because we could no longer afford them. This threat left my brothers and my mother utterly indifferent; they didn't believe it and in any case, they would have liked nothing better than a summer in the city. As for me, I was both thrilled and terrified at the prospect of being so poor, since I feared and longed to be living in dramatic circumstances. Nevertheless, those long months in the country that my mother and brothers grumbled over would recur punctually and inexorably each year, at my father's orders.

At some point I realized that the vacations in the mountains had become an intolerable bore for me as well. I knew then that my childhood was over. I no longer cared about grasshoppers and toads, and in the space of a few days I had read and reread the books I'd brought along. Besides, it was mortifying to sit alone and read. I thought I should have friends, but I had none. I had absolutely no idea how to pass the time. All at once I'd become a pessimist: the long empty afternoons promised nothing.

To make matters worse, I had to endure my boredom in isolation: my brothers had grown up and no longer came to the mountains with us, and my mother, oddly enough, no longer grumbled. She accompanied my father on his walks and joined him in extolling the beauties of nature and the purity of the air. I saw my parents as very old now. I felt a nameless boredom emanating from this contented old couple strolling side by side along the paths. I was invited to join them but didn't; to stroll in their company would have been embarrassing—clear and evident proof that I had no friends to take a walk with.

Every day I hoped it would rain, for if it rained I could stay inside, hidden from view. If it didn't rain, I was under orders to "go out in the fresh air," and I obeyed my parents out of time-honored submission. I would read in the fields. I would read, but with no pleasure. I listened to the crickets chirping; the dazzling, infinite peace of the summer afternoon was deafening. It seemed to promise something, but that promise was mysteriously meant for everyone except me.

Groups of boys and girls would pass by, wearing sneakers and carrying tennis rackets. I didn't know them, and couldn't join them because I was incapable of addressing a single word to them. They inspired a mortal envy. They enjoyed the supreme privilege of not having my parents, of being totally unlike me, not having the most remote connection to me. They enjoyed the supreme privilege of being other. Moreover they were going to play tennis and I didn't know how to play tennis. Tennis was a sport my father disdained. He considered it elitist. He approved only of challenging and risky sports like mountain climbing.

It suddenly seemed I was the only person in the world, apart from my parents, who had never set foot on a tennis court, and this absence of tennis in my life was a grotesque humiliation. I went down the list of the girls I knew in the city. They all knew how to play tennis or else they were learning from a "trainer," a professional coach. Once in a while my mother would absent-mindedly say, "It would be good for you to play tennis." And yet it never even crossed her mind to find a "trainer" for me. My father would have found it an absurd notion as well as an unnecessary expense. Whenever I passed a tennis court with my mother, I blushed and looked away. To ask for lessons was beyond me, since I had abruptly immured my most painful long-ings in silence. So my mother never knew that what I wanted most in the world was to stand on a tennis court in a white pleated skirt, holding a racket and saying the words "play" and "ready." I used to murmur those words to myself in secret, con-vinced they were the keys to happiness.

Later on, in high school, I did play tennis with my school-mates. I had an old racket dug up out of the cellar and a skirt that was neither white nor pleated; everything was all wrong. I played maybe a dozen times, not very well, and the thrill of say-ing "play" and "ready" proved flimsy indeed.

It was then, on those lonely vacations, that I began to hate the summer. My presence in the fields, on those brilliant after-noons, felt like a dark stain defiling the earth's felicity. I didn't find the world sad, I found it very beautiful, except that for some obscure reason I was forbidden to join in the celebration of its radiant days. And so I could only seek to love autumn, winter, twilight, rain, and night.

I discovered, later on, that I wasn't the only one to feel this way: it was a feeling shared by many. Many people, at some point in their lives, have felt as alienated and mortified by summer as I did, judged forever unworthy of reaping the harvest of the uni-verse. Many, like me, have hated the brilliance of the sky glaring over woods and fields. Many, like me, feel a sense of anguish at the first signs of summer, as if at news of disaster, for once again they are infused with the dread of being judged and con-demned.

We find ourselves rooted in place, with no means of escape. If alone, we instantly grasp the precise measure of our alone-ness. The usual rhythm of our days is broken. Our usual suffer-ings, relentlessly clarified by the sun's ruthless glare, become unbearable. Our life lies splintered at our feet. We feel driven to enumerate our every grief and failing. Summer's light, showing no mercy, illuminates our silence, our inert self amid its catastrophes old and new.

Before we know it we are sitting in the prisoner's dock—immobilized, annihilated, devastated, as if subjected to the third degree. No way to hide from ourselves or anyone else. No way to raise an arm to shield our face. We cannot answer any of the questions that are posed, we cannot perform any of the acts that are commanded. To be who we are is a crime worse than murder, and all the world proclaims that for such a crime, there can be no absolution. The old adolescent despair surges up again, that sudden sense of being called upon to be different, to be happy, but we are unable to heed the call.

We know from long experience that after the fifteenth of August the trial will be over. Gradually we'll slip back into a tranquil, shaded light, where we can murmur our own private, individual pardon. Patiently, we'll piece together our scattered ruins.

The days until the fifteenth seem endless. We loathe the empty city under the blinding sun, the empty movie houses showing horror films. We watch them unmoved, either because they're awful, or because as far as we're concerned we're already gripped by horror. But we loathe the crowded trains even more. Everyone is leaving town, everyone asks if we'll be leaving too. What to say? We are one of those who haven't the will either to leave or to stay.

August, 1971

misery in the beautiful, horrible city

For a few moments last Sunday, our first "austerity Sunday,"* it felt wonderful to walk lightheartedly down Via Quattro Fontane under the night sky, with no automobiles around. The city was all wind and stone and the air was frigid and odorless, as it is high up in the mountains.

But I couldn't quite experience a stroll in a city without cars as a legitimate, guiltless pleasure. One of the worst curses to have befallen us is that we cannot, for a single instant of our lives, feel ourselves to be legitimate and guiltless.

I realized, then, that my sense of well-being, walking in a city without traffic, was merely a physical well-being. It didn't yield any peace or tranquillity. Possibly never before had it been so clear as in last Sunday's silence, that peace and tranquillity, for us, are unattainable blessings. We are forever in a state of alarm, both for ourselves and for others. And the worst of it is that our fear on behalf of others springs not from some vital and generous part of our spirit, but from a quite cold, enervated, and ungenerous part. We remain fiercely self-involved in body and in

---

* For a period during the energy crisis of the early 1970's, automobiles were banned in Rome on Sundays.

spirit, and our fear for others is part and parcel of our self-involvement, becoming simply one more facet of it.

Last Sunday I thought, and maybe others did too, that it's not the cars that make our streets impassable, but something else. What that something else might be comprised of is hard to say. What our misery might be comprised of is hard to say. It has dwelt in us for years on end, yet we don't know what it is made up of. What we do know is that it sullies and pervades the streets even when the cars are absent.

Some people don't own cars and don't know how to drive. Generally they don't go about in Rome on Sundays. Those people thought, selfishly, that the Sunday without cars was a gift from the gods. Then they immediately felt guilty for having thought it. Needless to say, there is no thought that doesn't arouse some sense of guilt, either unconscious or explicit.

Other people, those who do drive cars, also have occasion to loathe them. No one can love cars when the city is full of them; everyone loathes them. We've inundated the streets with something it is impossible not to loathe.

To the avowed enemies of automobiles, those who don't own them or would be unfit to drive them in any case, the momentary physical well-being brought about by their absence suddenly seemed tremendously obtuse. We all realized we had expected that that single day could cure us of our malaise. That was an extremely short-sighted hope: the cars were with us in spirit just the same. Present or absent, they were indestructible. And in the end everyone felt a strange nostalgia for the city with its traffic: it was a truer reflection of our inner confusion.

Without cars, the city seemed naked. Naked, it was beautiful and appalling. We felt we could touch it. Some said it felt like a return to the postwar days. That wasn't so. In fact the city felt very different from the postwar days. At night, in the postwar era, every neighborhood in Rome took on the feel of a village, so that the whole city was like an enormous cluster of villages gathered together, each one curled up in a domestic, creaturely slumber, like the slumber of herds and poultry.

Today, nothing seems as distant and remote from Rome as the countryside, and in no way does the city evoke poultry or herds. No traces of stillness or animal life remain. Today the city is everywhere huge, everywhere mineral, and seems never to sleep; when it's empty, it feels dead. Last Sunday, stripped of automobiles, Rome by night was solemn and desolate, as spectral and inanimate as the craters of the moon.

We realized, moreover, how hard it is to recall postwar Rome in any detail. We realized how hard it is to recall the cities of our childhood, as they used to be. We automatically fill them with cars, even if back then the streets were vast and empty. To envision cities that are happily and peacefully empty, we have to envision ourselves as having been born and passing our lives in long-gone eras. And when fantasy transports us to those ancient, long-gone eras, we feel a sense of respite and liberation. Which means that only in fantasy can we conceive of tranquillity. Our memory cannot call forth tranquillity. Wherever it alights, in whatever segment of our lives, it drags along our selves as we are today, burdened with trailing anxieties.

Walking through the city stupefied by traffic, we can neither think nor look at our surroundings. Our relationship to the city is totally destroyed. What is curious and paradoxical is that we cannot reconstruct this relationship when the cars are gone. The city no longer weaves any connections with us. Even though we can finally see it and touch it, it just sits there: solitary, unwelcoming, impregnable.

Last Sunday we walked around thinking either of ourselves or of others. There was no way to forge a relationship with the city. We felt it as alien, unknown. We were in direct contact with our misery.

Our misery has a unique quality; we tend to think there has never been anything quite like it before. We tend to think the world has never known a misery of so general and universal a nature as ours. Our individual ills and sufferings breed within it and multiply, reaching dizzying, incalculable totals; there is hardly world enough and time to keep track of them in daily life. Our private misfortunes are not condemned or punished in the ordinary course of events; it is only we ourselves who judge them so severely. We have cluttered and enveloped our surroundings with engines and noise, a cunning way to avoid seeing how we live, or seeing too closely the distinct features, the colors and contours, of our misery. Then we promptly despised such cunning and mistook it for the misery itself.

When a crack appears in the reality we ourselves have constructed and layered with noise and engines, when it is borne in on us that this reality might not be so solid after all, then it stands stripped before our gaze; we grasp that the noise and the engines are not the source or the cause of our misery at all but rather a superficial layer, a symptom or a sign, not an element to be considered in isolation.

With this in mind, by the close of day last Sunday, our first "austerity Sunday," the absence of automobiles felt salutary and validating. True, our well-being was merely physical and we were in no way happier by their absence but even more insecure, frightened, and miserable. But it was possible at last to recognize the misery we were dealing with, and maybe even to illuminate it with words. Something had happened: it wasn't conducive to hope—hope doesn't seem to thrive in our soil—but it was conducive to truth.

December, 1973

fantasy life

In childhood and youth, as soon as we found ourselves alone and idle, we would start fashioning imaginary places, complete with stories and incidents in which we were the protagonists. We peopled these places and stories with characters, either invented or chosen from our daily life. In early childhood we favored invented people and felt we were constructing our scenarios for them. Real people, at that point, were of no importance.

Time and again, we've rooted around in our distant childhood to discover when we first began to fantasize. But we can't pinpoint the exact moment. As far back as we can recall, we find dreams.

Probably every child has his own term for fantasy. I called it "night talk." Actually I didn't fantasize only at night but during the day as well. But the word "night" must have evoked for me the secret and nocturnal quality of fantasy.

In my childhood fantasies, I was host to whole populations that swarmed through my solitary hours like an army of ants. They were partly my subjects, partly my accomplices in government conspiracies, partly my teasing, malevolent persecutors. I called them "the we's," since that was what they called themselves. They boasted shamelessly, flaunting their evil wishes in choruses of shrieks. They were very tiny, a tribe of swarming, vainglorious black dwarves. They could make me rage, weep, whisper and argue, but most of all their deafening shrieks made me laugh. For reasons I couldn't have explained, their existence could not be revealed to a soul.

Sometimes, walking down the street with my mother, I would begin fantasizing as if I were alone in my room. The "we's" would deafen me with their shrieking demands, and I would respond with gestures, grimaces, and whispers. When my mother asked why I was making such monkey faces, I was overwhelmed with shame. There was nothing I liked better than "night talk," but to entertain the "we's" on the street, in the presence of my mother, suddenly struck me as disgraceful and humiliating. I thought I was the only person in the world to harbor so peculiar, ridiculous, and humiliating a secret. I thought I was probably crazy.

Later on, the "we's" became tiresome: there were too many of them. I invented one person and gave him a very handsome face, thick, curly blond hair, and a Cossack-style shirt. I named him Prince Sergio. I gave him a sister, three brothers, a few bears, and a rather ferocious Alsatian dog. I also gave him several very sumptuous houses where he could hide out. He was very rich, but he was a refugee who had escaped from Russia with state secrets during the revolution. I loved his wandering, princely life. He was forever moving from one house to another, since he was being followed. I often phoned him the moment I was alone, pretending to hold a receiver in my hand. "Hello, is Prince Sergio there?" Sometimes he answered, and sometimes his sister, Vassilissa. Our romance lasted many years. To this day, I find myself recalling the words "Hello, is the prince there?" I seem to be wandering aimlessly through empty rooms, holding an old slipper in my hand.

After childhood I got bored with made-up people. It was much more rewarding to fill my dreams with real people.

For a long time, we think we must be the only one in the world
with a fantasy life. Later on we realize it's something lots of people have, maybe even everyone.

In childhood and youth, we loved to arouse pity, both in ourselves and in others: it yielded rich, voluptuous feelings. Feeling
sorry for ourselves and having others feel sorry for us made us
feel loved. We would murmur sympathetic words to ourselves at
great length. In old age, our compassion for ourselves is barren,
absentminded and arid, while the sympathy of others provokes
a strange mixture of gratitude and repulsion. Even the gratitude
is arid and absentminded. The repulsion is stronger. When others feel sorry for us, we turn away.

In childhood and youth, we loved to be envied. In old age,
the idea of inciting envy leaves us cold as ice.

In our youthful fantasies, pity and envy sprang up at our feet
like grass, and it felt wonderful to walk on that carpet of grass.
But above all we loved to inspire amazement. Amazement is the
opposite of indifference, and since in real life we were often
pained to meet with—or think we were meeting with—indifference, we loved to have people regard us with amazement, and
we strewed it all through our fantasies. In our fantasy life, we cultivated everything lacking, or in short supply, in our real life.

After childhood we gave up the swarming crowds; we gave up
piecing our fantasies together with scraps of sentimental ro-
mances, preferring the company of a small group of people chosen from real life and transported to fantasy. Only there, we
discovered, were we finally freed of our awkwardness. There, in
our daydreams, we finally managed to speak to those people
loud and clear, to form close and intimate connections, and to
rid ourselves of the sadness that had come over us at the end of
childhood, making us look back on that childhood as a lost and

blessed time. Now, in our fantasies, we rarely laughed out loud and only occasionally whispered, yet the room would be filled with laughter and whispering while we sat motionless, praying only that no one would come in. Our imaginary voice resounded in the silence of our mind, our imaginary gestures were graceful and free. We realized, then, how choked and impoverished our actual relationships were, how crude and stingy our gestures, how rare and faint our words. Comparing our fantasy life with real life, we found the former to be infinitely more fulfilling. And in its midst, we were free at last. But we were unable to bring any of that force and grace into our real life. Indeed the memory of the fantasy life, in which we had appropriated real people for our personal use, capriciously moving them around and wrenching them in and out of place like objects, made us even sadder, gawkier, and more cowardly in real life, in the presence of real people.

The goal of our existence, we believed, was to become in actuality the person we were in fantasy. We thought that by training ourselves to behave freely and courageously in fantasy, we would one day attain real grace and freedom. Our fantasy life seemed a kind of gymnastic training, by which we would finally learn a better way of being in the world. We were mistaken: in actual life, the memory of our fantasies weighed heavily on us. When we put them side by side, fantasy life and real life, their huge disparity sent chills down our spine.

Once transported to our dreams, real people kept their own characteristics, only in a paler, milder, less distinct form. They became gentler, always ready to agree with us, keenly attentive to our every bad mood or melancholy, easy to get along with, submissive, patient, and disposed to make every sacrifice on our behalf. Not only did we improve immensely in our daydreams, but others improved as well, and the very temperature of the air

was better, never too cold or too hot, so that we never sweated or
went numb with cold but were forever basking in a benign,
balmy atmosphere. The only disturbing notion was that all those
people we were using in our dreams might in real life have all
sorts of chores and worries and preoccupations; they might even
be having nervous fits or temper tantrums at the very moment
we were arranging their bodies in calm, smiling poses suitable
for temperate conversation. In their actual presence we felt a
kind of remorse, as if they had been exploited unawares, and as
if clouds of flies or mosquitoes might erupt from our dreams to
plague us all. And the fact that these people were totally igno-
rant of inhabiting our dreams was more troubling than reassuring, because for us the mind had a real existence, however
hidden; it existed and partook of the truth, and its secret, invisible nature rendered it even more insolent and distressing vis-à-
vis reality.

In the realm of dream, our constant fear of never being the
protagonist, of remaining always in a walk-on role, disappeared.
In the realm of dream we promptly and resolutely took center
stage in the universe. We kindled ardent and profound feelings
in everyone around us. The scenario of our eventful lives was enhanced by incredulous, bedazzled testimonies to our high and
extraordinary destiny. We chose one person from our real life to
stand alongside us as fellow protagonist, while others, those who
in reality inspired fear and veneration, became spectators or
were assigned bit parts. This filled us with a mad joy that felt
quite strange, insolent, possibly even criminal, but we wouldn't
have given it up for anything in the world. Nor would we have
revealed it to a living soul for anything in the world.

In childhood, we thought that above all, our fantasies should
conjure up and dwell on our own happiness. We dressed up in
elegant new costumes and frequented fantastic places—fabu-

lously opulent houses, parks and meadows with roving pea-
cocks, where astoundingly white sheep grazed and stupendous
horses galloped. After childhood, though, happiness began to
bore us. Our dreams took to brooding far more often on our
ruin. Our great dread in real life was to appear comic rather
than tragic; we dreaded that whatever fate had in store for us
might fall under the mask of comedy and not tragedy. In our
fantasies, therefore, we would offer our destiny the gift of great
and somber disasters. Dressed in mourning, we followed the fu-
neral cortege of both our parents, while people stroked our
poor, orphaned head. In reality, sitting at the dinner table with
our parents, we would recall how we had just buried them;
watching them eat and exchange their placid remarks, we would
think how firmly riveted to happiness our real life was, this life
in which the absence of funerals, indeed of any events at all, was
quite remarkable.

After childhood, more and more often our fantasies would
find us in the grip of complex, perilous situations, with no chance
of escape. We would be capsized in a torrent of calamities. We invented protracted illnesses—we had pneumonia and coughed
up blood—long exiles in the most depressing hospital wards,
heartrending partings from those we held most dear. We even
died. Stabbed in our very own doorway. Shot. Imprisoned and
visited by tearful friends as we lay on our filthy pallet, while outside the gallows awaited us, the tocsin rang out, and people
flocked from every direction to watch us die. For long spells, our
dreams were always the same. Once in a while we might alter
some small detail, changing the various friends who came to
weep or adding to their number, or altering a line in the script
here and there, perhaps our final serene words before being put
to death. For quite some time there was the gallows, then for a
good while it was the barricades. We couldn't account for the

changes in the scenario: they didn't feel like our own doing. The will to dream was our own, the choice of characters was definitely our own, but the scenarios and the events seemed beyond our control. It was we who invented them, but in obedience to some murky instinct compelling us to invent in this or that mode.

In childhood, our imaginary scenes and settings were richly colored, and we would linger over every tiny detail. We had to know what everyone was wearing, which animals were present, and how the furniture in the houses was arranged, not to mention the trees in the parks. Once the whole scene was set, we would fall into a trance, lost in contemplation as if on our knees, dazzled by the brilliance of the sky, the sumptuousness of the colors. After childhood our mode of dreaming changed utterly. All precision of detail was gone. Now the essential features were scantness of invention, swiftness, and tonelessness. Since we considered ourselves blessed with imagination, it seemed strange that the more brief and barren our fantasies were, the more stripped and unadorned the scenarios, the more joy they would yield; even if they were tragic and bloody, still their rhythm and pace were too swift to allow much room for a rich luxuriance of facts. The scenarios were unadorned because we no longer enjoyed lingering over colors and furnishings. Colors and furnishings were boring. If our blood flowed, it was colorless.

The episodes always started and ended at the same point, like a song on a record. They were always inconclusive; we would watch them trail off in the shadows like the tail of a fish. Even our death didn't signal a conclusion, because it was followed by bells, tears, and genuine outbursts of grief from those we had selected for precisely that purpose. Still, it was impossible to get beyond that inconclusive point. We would go back and repeat it all over again from the beginning. Despite the sameness of it all, we were never bored. A few very minor changes sufficed. We would emerge from our fantasies wide-eyed, dazed, unsatisfied, with the fleeting vision of that inconclusive ending.

We've often felt scorn for our fantasy life. Its path, we thought, strayed far from any intellectual choice. It strayed far from our moral life. It carried all the rubbish of our mind. There were times, in our fantasies, when we behaved generously: we could be charitable, heroic, ready for every sacrifice and martyrdom. But we could be bitchy, and acting bitchy gave us an unbridled joy. Our fantasy life clearly harbored our worst features: our cruelty, vanity, boastfulness, laziness. Our endless fantasies and our indulgence of them could only spread sloth and indulgence in the life of the spirit.

We sometimes wondered if there was any relationship between the fantasy life and the creative life. They inhabited the same realm, the realm of imagination. Moreover, they both grew and ripened in idleness and solitude.

In periods of creative activity, our fantasy life usually ceased to exist—usually, but not always. Creative activity required a profound silence, while the fantasy life resounded with whispers, voices, bursts of laughter. Also, we used to feel that in periods of creativity, our personal destiny should be a matter of indifference to us, and so it was distressing to find that that was not always the case. Sometimes we would take breaks, pausing in our work to invent scenarios as a gift for our destiny, or to amuse ourselves by long talks with imaginary interlocutors, carrying on our fantasy life as always, which we found an extremely base practice. We called it work, but it felt no different from idleness. The only discernible difference between our idle fantasy life and the creative life was that in the creative life our mind would buzz and sting as if crowded with needles and bees. Our fantasy life held no needles or bees: our mind was vacant, smoothly fluid. Lastly, the creative life produced or might produce work. The fantasy life was sterile and would never produce a thing. But frankly, in youth this was not an appreciable difference, since quite often what we called work didn't produce anything either.

All the same, we thought on occasion that if we hadn't had a fantasy life, we might not have found the path to the creative life, or it wouldn't have occurred to us to seek it. We never did manage to learn, in our fantasy life, the proper ways to behave in real life, but we did find a few random tools useful for the creative life: a special kind of attentiveness, a cast of mind at once authoritative and reverent in manipulating elements of reality. The creative life was the best thing we possessed, the fantasy life possibly the worst. But maybe they were blood relatives, inseparable one from the other.

There were times when our fantasy life anticipated and foreshadowed what would later happen in real life. But its predictions were a mockery. If years later we compared some of our inventions with our actual experience, the inventions resembled a crude caricature of what actually happened. At other times it was just the opposite. It was reality that made a mockery and caricature of our fantasies. A cruel, mocking caricature, compared to our mild, melancholy, vaporous fantasies.

Comparing our fantasies with actual events, we were sometimes astonished by what we had dared to conceive of, what delirious and boundlessly ambitious schemes had swirled within us. Never did we see ourselves in so grotesque a guise, nor laugh at ourselves so profoundly and so bitterly as when we studied the arabesques of our ambitious imaginings in the light of what actually happened. Our laughter was vast and shocking to our ears, reverberating as it did in the silence, lacerating and harrowing, because our ears alone could register its sound.

Over the course of our life we acquire a strong sense of the ridiculous. When we invent episodes for our destiny, we are hard put to forget that it is we who must live through them. In childhood and youth, when we abandoned ourselves to fantasy, we lost all sense of the ridiculous.

Growing old, we have no idea what will become of our fantasy life, our stubborn habit of dreaming, contracted in the farthest reaches of childhood. If in the course of our life we ever played the role of protagonist, now, in old age, we feel sure this will no longer happen. And no doubt in others' lives we'll play minor roles: witnesses, walk-ons, spectators. Not even in our secret fantasies will we play an essential part. Our every dream will be lightless. Impossible to turn on the light, the wires being frayed, impossible to build a stage in our ravaged theaters. This, we realize, must be old age. Making the gesture of turning on the lights and remaining in the dark.

In youth, we very seldom thought about growing old. When we did happen to think about it, we assumed old age would so totally transform us that we would be unrecognizable even to ourselves. We believed we would become resolute, sturdy, and totally tranquil. Our aged self was a stranger, and the fate of this stranger was none of our concern. Her face, her voice, her thoughts were all alien to us. In expectation of turning into this stranger, we prepared ourselves for a solid, quiet old age, as one prepares oneself for a long and comfortable therapeutic stay at a health spa. Instead, old age knocked us over like a gust of wind. It battered at our errors, our ineptness, our rashness, incoherence, and frailty. It brought no remedy for our failings. They are even more apparent to us, and more unforgivable toothers. Nor have we become strangers. Our essential nature has not changed in the least. It is still we ourselves who must endure old age: its transformations of body and spirit have been enormous and profound, but not such as to render us unrecognizable. The deepest core of our spirit is exactly the same. We observe the transformations and ravagings of mind and body, but we observe them with the same foolish eyes of always.

We think that gradually we shall become hard and strict with ourselves, implacable in forbidding any flights of fancy or intellectual frivolity. We'll close the door on the fantasy life, the way you close the doors and the shutters to go to sleep.

But instead, in idle moments we still set about inventing imaginary places, out of ancient habit. Wearily, we sit down. Our imagination has grown timid, cold, cautious. In real life we may be somewhat less timid, but now it's our imagination that is timid. What are we to do now, in idle moments, with such a cold and timid imagination, shut up in imaginary rooms where nothing more happens?

In old age, we're afraid of forgetting what happiness was all about. We think our vision of the world will be forever incomplete now, forever murky and truncated. There was a moment in our life when we grasped that never again would we be happy; destiny might hold all sorts of things in store, but not happiness, not anymore. A moment like that draws a dividing line in our life, a deep, black furrow. To remember happiness, we have to look at the stretch of land beyond that furrow. Our memories remain. But memories offer only a few scattered traces of happiness. We find it hard to reconstruct a complete image of it. The feelings we remember seem too exalted and passionate, compared to happiness. We're afraid of possibly forgetting the real nature of happiness, that state we dwelt in as in our natural element, so natural, so self-evident, and so real that in the end we even made bad use of it.

In memory, what is present and what is lost are inextricably linked. The same faraway red sun shines on our every distant memory, whether of grief or happiness. It makes each trivial moment of our past precious and luminous. It is impossible for us, ever again, to enjoy the privilege of living in that realm, amid that splendor. It is so far away that we can't even summon up the warmth of its rays on our cold sands.

When we were in love, our fantasy life took on immense significance. Dreams blossomed in our mind like the first spring flowers on a tree, and we scattered them over our destiny in profusion. We felt rash, bestowing this gift, for we understood that our destiny was at a delicate point where even a single flower might damage it. And yet we couldn't turn our mind to stone. We couldn't stop it from blossoming.

In old age, we're afraid of forgetting what love was all about. We do remember that it could come in two modes. It could come suddenly, setting fire to the world. Or it could come almost unnoticed, the color of air. Love was either like air or like fire.

When it was like air, we could recognize it by certain signs. The swiftness of the hours; our light breathing; the great pleasure we took in performing the smallest and most banal tasks, straightening out a drawer or going out to mail a letter—tedious, numbing tasks that ordinarily, on our gray days, bored us to death. Our fantasy life stayed the same, or was even more crowded with incident. But it kept within the bounds of reason. We felt strong, intelligent, calm.

When love was like fire, time was neither slow nor fast: it no longer existed. We could spend hours entranced, watching the world burn. What others said or did or experienced, we found suffocating; we felt we were breathing and swallowing ashes, practically smothering in ashes. Our mind, or what remained of our mind, drifted dazedly between flames and ashes. We couldn't do anything except daydream. But our fantasy life was wildly irrational, spinning madly on turbulent ground, and in our rare moments of lucidity it felt very dangerous, as everything is dangerous in the presence of fire. It wasn't depicting unusual or prodigious events, but rather simple, lifelike ones, and for that very reason it was dangerous—too close to reality, trying to clasp it tight and force it into the shapes of fantasy. The retaining wall between reality and dream was cracked and collapsing. We would find ourselves saying and doing exactly what we had said and done in fantasy. Our words sounded sharp and shrill, our actions were senseless and grievous. We thought our fantasy life was the worst enemy of our real life. It was our dreaming that had made us awkward, solitary, and wretched. It was our dreaming that had made us morbid and paralyzed, bloating our spirit with such huge clouds that it was too heavy to move freely in the real world.

Looking back on our youth, we remember living through whole long love stories as if on two paths, an imaginary path lush with happy events and a real and desolate path where we knew only sorrow. We suspect that if we hadn't known such happy events in fantasy, the sorrows of real life might not have been so desolate and profound.

Our fantasy life, with its profusions of happiness, brought us bad luck. It colonized our actual life, plundering whole provinces and regions. It was as if someone had decreed that since we had already lived through such a happy story in fantasy, there was no need for us to relive it in reality. Looking back on those happy imaginings, we are surprised to discover how lifelike and attainable they were, full of words and incidents that felt real. The only unreal thing about them is that they never happened.

For long years our fantasy life was calm. Every so often we might glance coolly and absently at its blossoms, drained of color beyond the windowpane of our hurried mornings. Walking down the street alone, now and then we might erect a hasty gallows and climb up, to die with marvelous serenity. Or fling ourselves under a moving train and save a few lives. From the offhandedness of these scenes, it was clear they were superfluous. We were tossing a dash of martyrdom, a dash of blood, into a life devoid of martyrdom. Our fantasies didn't spring from melancholy but from joy. They weren't a refuge; they were a vacation.

So when we try, in old age, to remember what happiness was like, we remember it as a time of calm fantasies. A time when we had natural, limpid relations with others. A time when we never wondered if we were or would be protagonists. We felt physically located in the center of the universe, or rather we occupied the only point in the universe that was right and fitting for us to occupy.

It was a time when silence and leisure nurtured ideas, not privation and not longings. Our fantasy life was at rest. The occasional imaginary dialogues with people who didn't much matter, the occasional scenes of death and glory, of trumpets blaring and bells ringing and flags waving, were the light, happy blossoms we carried around with us, in our happiness.

In old age, we think of everything we have had and will never have again, of everything we've done and will never do again, as well as everything we have not been and never will be. In this way, we come to know inexorability. In youth, we knew it only in times of calamity; our daily life was the opposite of inexorable. At the first glimpse of approaching calamity, we would offer our destiny the gift of possible change. When we were bruised by misfortune, our fantasy life would rush in to soothe us the minute we were alone. It thronged our solitary paths with friends; it filled our empty days with promise; voices and whispers rose up out of the silence; even though we alone were uttering the questions and answers, these imaginary dialogues were so comforting that they seemed to come from outside. In old age, inexorability has settled into our daily life. To know the inexorable in daily life means that our mind intimately embraces our death—real, not imaginary.

In old age, we sometimes get the notion of replacing certain facts in our past by other facts, that is, of emending our lived reality. We realize, then, that we are no longer inventing for the future but for the past, and that in emending the past we are crossing over into a world of things we perceive and know to be impossible. In youth, our fantasy life never crossed over into impossibilities, for whatever unusual and prodigious happenings we might conceive of, somewhere within them always lurked a hope or a thirst or a need or a plea or a genuine longing. In old age, when we emend our past, we plunge abruptly into a fantasy life devoid of hope and devoid of thirst, devoid of any pleading or longing, because one doesn't plead or long for what is impossible—or more accurately, one does so with the definite sense of desiring, invoking, and touching the void. So we turn away from those fantasies and throw out every emendation. We have a kind of allegiance to whatever has happened. And this allegiance to what has happened leads us to a place that is the polar opposite of our long, drawn-out fantasy life, a place where everything is clear, inexorable, and real.

May, 1974

IV **ginzburg** wrote the following impassioned declaration in response to the storm of controversy in Italy and the Italian press over the Serena Cruz adoption case in 1989. As she notes, the case tore the country apart, dividing friends and allies along ideological lines. Her purpose, as stated in an Author's Note, is "to bear witness to my solidarity" with all the families who were devastated by inhumane and generalized application of the adoption laws—inhumane precisely because generalized.

The selections below amount to slightly less than half of the original book, which is a brilliant example of polemic filtered through a highly literary sensibility. The omitted passages pertain to technicalities of Italian adoption laws and practices, or are lengthy quotes from leading intellectuals and journalists, or summaries of other cases that outraged Ginzburg, cases of children being snatched from their homes without warning for unjustifiable cause (the parents' poverty or unusual marital arrangements, for instance), or of wrongful charges of parental abuse.

The issues raised by the Serena Cruz case were the perfect challenge for one of Ginzburg's temperament and inclinations. She spent her life painstakingly unraveling the meaning and implications of individual experience, both personally and politically. Inevitably she would find the abstractions so dear to the legal and social work professions profoundly offensive, especially when applied to a specific family. To readers of her novels and essays, her loathing of legalism and bureaucracy and the rigidities they produce could come as no surprise. Nor would her scorn of the "lukewarm" mentality, and the resulting obfuscation and debasement of language which she so deplores.

The Italian adoption laws are in the process of being revised, partly along the lines Ginzburg suggests, and certainly her book was instrumental in bringing about needed change. According to the new provisions, the principle that a child has a right to be raised in its own family would be strengthened, and the law and its application made more flexible. Social service agencies would no longer be permitted to remove a child from its family simply because of poverty, and families would be notified in advance of pending investigations or legal action. All parties involved would be entitled to legal representation, provided by the state if necessary.

However, these new rulings are not yet final, and some critics say they are superficial and do not go far enough. Obviously they cannot undo the damage already done to the Giubergia family.

As far as I could discover, Serena Cruz's whereabouts after she left the Giubergias were never made public, and none of the Italian journalists I consulted knew what happened to her.

serena cruz, or the
meaning of true justice

*I would thou wert cold or hot. So then because
thou art lukewarm, and neither cold nor hot,
I will spue thee out of my mouth.*

REVELATION 3: 15-16

I

What follows is the story of Serena Cruz as I learned it from
the newspapers and from scattered hearsay. Her adoptive
parents, who were judged to be illegal, give an entirely different
version, which I will relate further on. But I offer here the version I found in the papers, which set me thinking along certain
lines. To follow the thread of my thoughts and feelings along the
way, I shall limit myself to what I read last spring, in the month
of March [1989] to be precise, when the discussion and debate
over the Serena Cruz case first began.

Here is the story given in the papers:

Serena Cruz was born in Manila, in the Philippines, on May
20, 1986. She was discovered in a garbage can, barely breathing.
It is not clear how her date of birth was established. Evidently

[195]

whoever found her determined that she was just a few hours old. Or perhaps her mother, who didn't want her and had abandoned her, was traced. The child was entrusted to public welfare and sheltered in an orphanage.

A year and a half later, toward the end of 1987, Francesco Giubergia, a railroad worker from Racconigi, arrived in Manila. He and his wife had lost a son some years earlier and couldn't have any more children. Afterward, they had adopted a baby boy in Manila. Now they wished to adopt another child, so that the boy already living with them in their house in Racconigi could enjoy having a brother or sister from his native country.

They had adopted that first child, called Nazario, when he was seven months old. At the time, he weighed a little over seven pounds and was sick with a lung ailment—a pulmonary infection, the doctors explained—and bone decalcification. Because of this, other couples had rejected him. The Giubergias took him. Once the necessary adoption procedures were completed, they brought him to Italy, to Racconigi, where he made a complete recovery. Now he was three and a half and doing well.

When Francesco Giubergia returned to Manila in 1987, alone this time, someone told him about a baby girl in an institution, in wretched condition. He visited and found her crowded together with hundreds of other children. When he saw her, he vowed to get her out of there as soon as possible.

Francesco Giubergia was a man of humble station. Had he been rich, he and his wife would have established residence in the Philippines for eighteen months, as Filipino law now requires of foreigners wishing to adopt a child—a stipulation urged by Cory Aquino. It was not in force earlier, when they adopted the first child. Now it was. How could a railway worker from Racconigi and his wife spend eighteen months in the Philippines? He didn't have enough money. His wife was a nurse in USL.* They would both lose their jobs. He was also told that if the baby girl remained in the institution much longer she would die. On January 7, 1988, Francesco Giubergia went to the Italian Embassy in Manila and declared the child to be his daughter, born of his relationship with an eighteen-year-old girl from Manila, Marlene Vito Cruz, a midwife's apprentice. He had the child entered on his passport.

He handed over four documents to the Italian Embassy: the baby's birth certificate, which said she was born at 17 Largit Street in Caloocan, a neighborhood in the Maypajo section on the outskirts of Manila, to Francesco Giubergia, 35, Italian, state employee, and Marlene Vito Cruz, 18, unmarried. An acknowledgement of paternity. A statement by the mother affirming her wish to give up the baby, certified by a notary named Sulpicio Benigno. A certificate from a local court attesting to the qualifications of the notary, Sulpicio Benigno.

That was the newspaper account.

The Giubergias, as I said, give a different version: During his first trip to Manila, Francesco Giubergia met a girl and had sexual relations with her. When he went back the second time, it was not to adopt simply any baby, but to take his own daughter home with him, as the young mother had requested. He is now able to produce additional documents confirming that the child is his daughter. It was his mistake not to take the blood test as the judges ordered. Now he says he is willing to take it. His behavior with the judges was naïve and inept, he says, but there was no deception on his part.

On January 13 Francesco Giubergia returned to Racconigi with the child. Serena Cruz was then twenty months old. The other

* Unità Sanitaria Locale—a public health clinic, branch of the National Health Service.

child, Nazario, was there. The fact that he too was Filipino made everything easier. In her new home, Serena could see a face something like her own, like the faces she had been seeing all along. And so it was easier for her to understand and accept the rest.

Her name was entered in the town registry as Serena Cruz Giubergia.

She was a big baby, with a big belly. Her adoptive mother, knowing she was not well, had pictured her as tiny and frail. Instead she seemed fairly robust. Actually, as they and the doctors soon realized, she was bloated. She had wide eyes, round cheeks, and thick black bangs. Her adoptive mother noticed that her ears were pierced, an odd feature in a child whom surely no one had ever paid much attention to.

In Racconigi the doctors found that she had perforated eardrums, a vaginal infection, and lice in the cavities of her ears.

During the trip the child had grown fond of her father and at first she rejected her mother. But this lasted only a few days. Very soon her mother became the center of her universe.

She learned Italian quickly. At first they would hear her constantly repeat a word from her own language, *tamanà*. But once when her father said *tamanà* to her, she got upset and hid under the table. Apparently *tamanà* was some kind of command or prohibition.

Those twenty months in the orphanage had made her an anxious child. She had nightmares, phobias, peculiar habits. She would hunt for food in bags of garbage. She didn't want to sleep in a bed, only on the floor. She wanted to wash her hands all the time, as if she was afraid of never being clean enough. She would start with fear each time the doorbell rang. Her adoptive parents tried to reassure her and foster new habits. Everyone who knew them said they were excellent parents, ready to make any sacrifice so that their children would lack for nothing. Since they both worked, they hired a babysitter. A year and a half went by. Serena

Cruz loved her parents and was loved dearly by them. She loved her brother. She was a healthy, sturdy little girl now, though at times she still had nightmares, phobias, and anxieties. Everyone in Racconigi knew her. Everyone saw them as a happy family.

The Giubergias' small two-story house, which I later visited, is on a quiet street lined with similar houses and surrounded by countryside. It has a small garden. The children would spend whole days playing in the garden—two happy children who got along well. Serena was the assertive one; the boy had a more timid nature.

The details about the pierced ears, the perforated eardrums, and *tamanà* I didn't read in the papers but learned from the Giubergias themselves during my recent visit, which I shall describe later on.

The Juvenile Court learned of this child who had arrived from abroad and for whom no adoption papers had yet been submitted. On January 23, 1988, the Giubergias were summoned to court. Rosanna Giubergia appeared and said her husband was not feeling well. She told of an adulterous liaison her husband had had in Manila. Francesco Giubergia was summoned again for the twenty-nineth of the same month, and appeared.

He said the child was his daughter, as he had already told the Italian Embassy. He had had relations with a girl when he was in Manila before, to adopt the first child. Later on, in a phone call from the girl, he learned he was the father of a baby daughter. He hadn't gone there right away because he didn't have enough money for the trip. Once he had the money he went and brought the child back to Italy. Her birth mother didn't want her. She was very young and very poor. That was his account.

Rosanna Giubergia was summoned to court again, without her husband, and asked how many times her husband had slept with the girl. She said she didn't know.

In February, Francesco Giubergia applied to have Serena, his illegitimate daughter, officially listed as a member of his family.

The Juvenile Court ordered that he take a blood test. On the appointed day, Francesco Giubergia did not show up.

He had hired a lawyer, and this lawyer claimed that the blood test could not be required because the child had been acknowledged by both biological parents, even the mother. Later on he changed lawyers. The new lawyer asked for a postponement. The new lawyer challenged the Juvenile Court's jurisdiction in the matter of the blood test. The Court rejected his challenge and once again demanded the test. Francesco Giubergia did not appear. He subsequently claimed he hadn't received the new summons until it was too late. Thus the summer passed.

On October 27 the prosecuting attorney of the Juvenile Court "on the assumption that Serena would in the future inevitably be removed from the Giubergia family (given the almost certain falsity of identification), requests that the child be placed in a foster family, obviously a family other than the Giubergias."

On November 7 the court grants the prosecuting attorney's request.

On November 17 the Giubergias are summoned to court and informed that they cannot keep the child. Only at that point, they say, were they alarmed. Before that, they hadn't thought there was any intention of actually taking her away. The court clerks they had dealt with had always seemed cordial and well disposed. That is what they say. They look back on that day, November 17, as a terrible day....

In the opinion of the judges, Francesco Giubergia had lied in claiming the child was his daughter, and there was no familial relationship between him and Serena. Therefore, in their opinion, he had *failed to notify* the authorities. But the law says failure to notify *may* lead to the forfeiture of guardianship of the child. The judges ruled as if it said *must.*

Not one of the judges ever bestirred himself to go and see the child. Only two doctors from USL went to see her, and both testified that the adoptive parents were taking good care of the child and her health was fine. Nor did the court-appointed guardian ever go to see her.

The fact that during those fourteen months not one of the judges or the guardian ever made a move to see her in the Giubergia household strikes me as outrageous and inexplicable.

She was seen by Professor Vittorino Andreoli, a psychiatrist called in by the Giubergias. He spent an entire day at their house and wrote a long report which was promptly submitted to the judges. He said the child suffered from phobias and nightmares. To remove her from the home she had been living in for fourteen months would be extremely dangerous. However, Andreoli was acting on the Giubergias' behalf. Then how come no court psychologist was called in to verify the truth of Andreoli's report?

On March 7 all of Racconigi, a town of 10,000 people, goes on strike. Stores, restaurants, bars are all closed. "In the name of true justice," the entire town, including the parish priest and the mayor, demands in unison that Serena remain with her adoptive parents, in her own home.

A Serena Cruz Committee is set up in Racconigi. In the town hall, people sign petitions proclaiming solidarity with the Giubergias. The newspapers give the affair prominent coverage. More Serena committees are organized all over Italy and thousands of people sign petitions.

The President of the Republic intervenes with the judges. The judges, "standing shoulder to shoulder," warn him not to interfere with their actions.

Why stand shoulder to shoulder? Why not go to Racconigi instead and see how this child is doing with the parents they judge to be illegal? Wasn't it their strict duty to go there, before assuming such a grave responsibility and making a decision that by their own admission they found painful?

On March 17 Rosanna Giubergia Gaveglio, the unlawful adoptive mother, tells Serena she will be taking her to a nursery school where she can play with other children. The social workers who came early that morning gave orders that Nazario should be shut up in his room and told nothing. Rosanna Giubergia dresses Serena; on her back she puts a little knapsack in the shape of a bear, recently purchased. She carries her in her arms to the province's public shelter, as ordered. She obeys, fearing police intervention. Police officers swarm around the community building. "Worse than if we were the Red Brigade," she would recall later. On seeing her enter with the child, the officers lower their heads as if they are ashamed to be there. Once inside the building, Serena shrieks and cries desperately, clinging to her mother. She wants to go home. The social workers tear her from her mother's arms. They take her into another room and tell the mother to go home. She can return later on to see the child, they say, whenever she wants. Rosanna Giubergia goes home in tears. They lied to her, for they do not let her see the child again. Not her, nor the brother, nor the father.

An acquaintance of the Giubergias who heard the desperate screams from the street remembers to this day the harrowing noise, which went on for hours.

The mother has to explain to Nazario, who sees her return alone, that Serena won't be sleeping at home that night. The next day, again she has to give some explanation. I know it's not your fault if she doesn't come back home, the boy says. It's because of those ladies who came and had coffee.

When she entered the public shelter, Serena was wearing earrings. Her mother had bought them for her, since she had pierced ears. She had a little gold chain around her neck, a gift from her grandmother, Francesco Giubergia's mother, who also lives in Racconigi, on a small street not far from their house. Serena was very fond of these trinkets. In the shelter they were immediately taken away. She must keep nothing that could remind her of her past.

Serena stayed in the shelter, which was quickly invaded by a horde of journalists, only eight hours. At night she was carried off to another shelter whose location was kept secret.

Don Aldo Marengo, the parish priest of Racconigi, learned several days later that the child had cried incessantly and hysterically. He learned that a pediatrician, when informed of this, suggested that the social worker put a few drops of Valium in Serena's soup. After that evening, various other tranquilizers were administered to calm her. Later on, the parish priest would deny any such rumors: he had never heard anything of the sort.

On March 21 the Giubergias appeal the ruling. Francesco Giubergia asks that the child be returned to him in foster care. Without her family around her, the defense argues, surely she is terribly upset. Any child would be upset. But Serena Cruz more than the ordinary child, because, as Professor Vittorino Andreoli's report states, she is very troubled; she has phobias and nightmares as a result of the neglect and deprivations suffered during her first year in the Manila orphanage.

On March 31 the appeal is denied. The judges say it would have been granted only if new facts had been presented, for instance, if the child had shown genuine signs of trauma in her new situation. So in effect the judges admit that they might have ruled otherwise, had they thought it fitting. They admit it was not impossible. It was quite possible to rule otherwise: they chose not to.

The child showed no signs of grief, according to the judges. So said the social workers who took care of her, as well as the psychologist and the doctor who saw her in her new environment. They even sent along audiovisual documentation. She was eating well and playing with the other children. Not once had she asked for her mother.

This we find hard to believe. As far as the audiovisual documentation, it proves nothing. Obviously a child may eat and play and be in despair a moment later. What the parish priest originally said he heard seems far more accurate, more plausible, and more normal.

More plausible, more normal, and even less alarming. For in fact it is well known that a child's semblance of indifference in painful circumstances is a very bad sign. Let us hope, then, that Serena cried and screamed day and night, the way normal children always cry and scream when separated from their mothers.

As we have said, not only did the judges fail to see her in the Giubergia household; the various psychologists later consulted by the court didn't see her there either, nor did any of the people responsible for deciding her destiny. A court psychologist interviewed on television by Enzo Biagi said she had seen her only *afterward*, when she was already in the public shelter. She said she found her in good spirits, playing and eating normally, and seemingly unaware of her parents' and brother's absence....

"Serena is better off now," the judges proclaim in chorus. Now? In the shelter she was brought to? Better off than with the Giubergias? How can the judges know this, if they never saw her before?....

She is better off, the judges said, because the Giubergias, frightened and guilt-ridden, had an "anxiety-producing" relationship with her. Let us suppose that the relationship was "anxiety-producing." How could a child with phobias, tremors, and nightmares, raised in an "anxiety-producing" relationship, possibly be cured as if by magic the moment she is away from home? Who could believe this? As for all that "uninterrupted and peaceful" sleep, how can one help but think she was stuffed with drugs?

Either the Giubergias had an "anxiety-producing" relationship with her, whose long-term symptoms could hardly vanish in the space of a few hours, since the damage from any such relationship is not so readily curable. Or else, as the townspeople who saw her every day attest, they were bringing her up well, trying to reassure her and help her overcome her difficulties, which made her an essentially strong and healthy child despite her phobias and nightmares. That the separation from her brother and her parents was devastating to her heart and soul is beyond a doubt. One needn't be a psychologist to grasp that. The grief of that blow and its consequences, however, will be revealed only over the course of many years. The *long-range perspective* the judges refer to means imagining Serena fifteen or twenty years from now.

Her apparent indifference to the separation—described with notable satisfaction by the court psychologists—her calm and nonchalance, if authentic, are a sign not of health and stability but rather of self-control and dissimulation. They indicate her ability to hide her state of mind, to discipline and conceal her anguish and desolation. We must bear in mind, however, that those psychologists were looking at a child *they had never seen before.*

Let us suppose that the Giubergias' relationship with the child was indeed *anxiety-producing.* Suppose the house was dense with shadows and tension. The judges never saw that house, but they pictured it as plunged in gloom. Still, they loved the child, and loving her as they did, they were happy with her. It is possible to be simultaneously happy, anxious, and fearful. Guilt-ridden and happy at once. True affection cannot be opaque and gloomy. True affection is limpid, and clears the air.

In truth, how many households or families are without anxieties or fears or guilt from various sources, whether overt or secret? Do the Turin judges know many such households, many such blessed families?

Francesco Giubergia offered to go to jail, if only the child might be spared and left at home in peace. To the best of our knowledge, he has never admitted that he lied. To the best of our knowledge he admitted only to handling things in a confused and clumsy way. The newspapers reported that he asked to go to jail. His request was not granted.

If they consider him guilty and if he himself requested it, I can't see why they didn't send him to jail. Because, someone told me, to fine him or sentence him to a few months in prison would be neither significant nor exemplary enough. In the eyes of the world, only depriving him of the child would suffice. Or, as one of the judges commented, he wasn't sent to jail because he and his wife had already suffered a great deal and had realized the error of their ways. This sudden and unlooked-for mercy suddenly lavished on two people whose daughter they had snatched away, I find bizarre in the extreme.....

II

It goes without saying that lies and deception can be dangerous for the adoption process. To overlook them can create a dangerous precedent. Illegal adoption practices are frightful. The buying and selling of children is frightful. In this case there was no buying and selling, the judges themselves acknowledged. Still, there was an illegality, they say, a fraud.

But precisely because judges must be so wary of creating a precedent, shouldn't they be equally wary of being driven to ruthlessness? In the face of a risky situation, yes, one must take courage, one must hone and perfect one's tools and focus the gaze sharply on the future. Nevertheless it is wrong to plead fear as an excuse for relinquishing an acute focus on the present, the place we are in right now. It is wrong to conjure up abstract images that obliterate all sense of the present in its concrete reality and uniqueness.

Would we rather risk a thousand abstract images, called to mind as abstractions, or endanger and ultimately strike to the heart one real person, right now, right before our eyes—one defenseless child? Would we rather protect the images in our head or protect a single flesh-and-blood reality? That is the issue. Which do we choose?

Granted that Francesco Giubergia's deception, if it was one, could be dangerous. Let us assume it was a deception. Let us assume everything took place as the judges claimed and as the press reported.

Granted, it was dangerous. And being dangerous, it was serious as well. And yet looking at it in context, the broadest possible context, I cannot find it truly serious. If we set it against the panorama of all the things that go on in Italy today, if we place it alongside the ignoble, vile and sinister frauds that are committed daily for vile and base motives, then this man's crude deception, if it was one, appears slight. Bear in mind that he was told the child was dying and he had to act quickly if he wanted to save her. He didn't buy her. Buying and selling children is vile, but of this he is innocent—the judges themselves say so. If he lied, he lied to save time. He lied thoughtlessly and recklessly, but his motives were generous. In every fraud, even in every crime, the judges obviously take into account many factors at once: the people involved, the motivations, all the minute details, the events leading up to and following the act. But above all they consider character and motivation. At least they should. I don't know if they always do. Here, however, it seems the judges focused solely on the lie and deception, ignoring or disregarding all the rest. Shrewd operators cannot be allowed to go scot-free, they said. But Giubergia was no shrewd operator. He was anything but a shrewd operator. It's not hard to imagine why, if he began to lie, he had to persist in his lie. He got tangled in a mass of thorns and clung to these thorns, unable to extricate himself.

And once again, remember that he was convinced he was acting in the interests of the child.

The end doesn't justify the means, as we all know. Even the end of saving a child from suffering does not technically justify breaking the law. But those words, "the end doesn't justify the means," can be taken in the opposite sense. The end of protecting all children does not justify a cruel act against one defenseless, innocent, uncomprehending child.

The end doesn't justify the means: in essence, neither the Giubergias are justified, if they lied, nor the judges. But we must weigh the gravity of the illegal act against that of the cruelty marshaled to strike down an innocent person. We must compare the gravity of the illegal act done out of thoughtlessness—and therefore more understandable—with the gravity of the cruelty used against an innocent person—and therefore ruthless and incomprehensible. We must ask ourselves which action is more just, in the light of true justice. In the case of Serena Cruz, the judges turned their backs on this light. They moved in darkness.

Let us assume, as the judges claim, that Francesco Giubergia lied to the authorities and was not Serena's biological father. But is there really so great a difference between being a biological father or not? When a man takes upon himself, and in the eyes of the world, the sober commitment to be a father to a child, does it make any great difference whether he and this child are bound by blood ties?

People say the Giubergias persisted in their lies for too long, until the judges became exasperated and ruled as they did.

But aren't those judges duly sworn never to yield to anger? No matter who provokes them, no matter what the circumstances? If not, then what kind of judges are they?

The judges say: Because the Giubergias lied about the child, we find them unworthy to bring her up. They are immoral and not fit to be her mother and father. Living with them, the child would grow up surrounded by lies.

But if the Giubergias lied, they lied to the judges. It is quite possible that one might lie to a judge and yet be an excellent parent to one's child.

Once Serena was grown, it wouldn't have been so difficult to explain the events of her early childhood. Where is the great difficulty? As an adult, she would have understood.

Meanwhile, what in God's name did all the social workers and functionaries tell her in the public shelter, to explain why her family had suddenly vanished and why she wasn't being taken home? How many lies did they tell her?

If we consider the facts in a purely moral context, why is it worse to lie to a judge than to a child?

Marlene Vito Cruz, the girl who in the documents is shown to be Serena's birth mother, was traced in Manila. Several reporters made inquiries about her and her family, a large and poor family living on the outskirts of Manila. Marlene Vito Cruz is now seventeen, not eighteen as the documents state. She says she has never given birth to any child. Nevertheless, if the child is now three, she must have been fourteen at the time. It happens. It does happen, but it didn't happen to her. So she says. She never abandoned a child in a garbage can. She doesn't know Mr. Giubergia, indeed this is the first time she ever heard that name. Her father said that the child is better off in Italy in any case. They already have a houseful of children—his own, with various wives. The papers reported this last spring. The girl might well have kept the truth to herself.

Last spring, the Serena Cruz case split Italy in half. One half found the court's decision fair and unobjectionable, the other half found it unjust and inhumane. Every day the papers ran articles expressing contradictory views.

When the matter came up in conversation, I would find myself unexpectedly agreeing with unlikely people and disagreeing with people who I was sure must share my feelings. I had the strong and distinct sense that an injustice had been done, that an unfortunate child had been sacrificed for a captious legal principle, and that a nuclear family had been devastated and trampled underfoot for the sake of an abstract principle. I still have this strong and distinct sense even though I have wondered, at times, if I might be wrong. But the feeling is stronger than right or wrong. People tell me that the law is the law and must be respected at all costs. *Dura lex sed lex.** But it seemed to me then, and still seems today, that laws can sometimes be flawed and deficient, and at times even be poorly understood and poorly interpreted. I also have strong doubts that the words *dura lex sed lex* are fixedly and incontestably true. Laws need not always be

---

* "The law is harsh, but it is the law." A principle of classical Roman law.

harsh. They need to be just. And those who enforce them must furnish them with eyes and ears, to perceive clearly when firmness is required, and when tolerance and understanding. Above all, laws cannot be used as a noose to strangle people. They must be used rather in the service and aid of humanity.

I found myself in disagreement with people I love and esteem. I cannot and never will see things as they do. They say there are millions and millions of defenseless, innocent children who are victims of swindles and trafficking and other illegal acts, and these millions of children must be protected. But I believed, and still do, that it is unjust to harm one child, to tear her from her parents' arms, be they legal or illegal, in order to protect millions of abstract children, children without faces or names. These faceless children can be protected tomorrow. Meanwhile, today, let us protect just one, the one whose name and face and identity we know.

In a number of scornful and mocking newspaper articles, people who said what I am now saying were labeled *Big Mama Italy*. I fail to grasp why the maternal instinct should be scorned or mocked. It is a natural instinct, with nothing comical about it. It is shared by men as well as women. Even men have a mother inside them. There is nothing comical about mothers, nothing contemptible or base or irrational. We were also labeled *Heart and Tears Italy*, and mocked and derided on that score. But I would like to know how human destiny can possibly be regarded without a heart, and without tears.

Raving Mad Italy was another name for us. While the other Italy was called *Rational Italy*—the only one that had a legitimate right to speak.

Dura lex sed lex. But if we read the law again, we find that the words *dura lex* do not truly apply. Remember that the law says, "the absence of notification *may* lead to unfitness to obtain the adoption." The judges acted as if it said *must*. So the harshness does not derive from the law. The law permitted the judges to act otherwise.

Let us also recall the words of Attorney General Vassalli: "The judges were not bound by law to separate Serena from the Giubergia family."

Last spring, the judges of the Turin Juvenile Court received anonymous letters containing death threats: "You must restore Serena Cruz to her adoptive parents." An anonymous letter was even sent to Attorney General Giuliano Vassalli, who struggled so hard to have the child returned to the Giubergias. On April 6, a rudimentary bomb, burnt out by the night's rain, was found in the offices of a Dutch airline that provides direct flights to the Philippines, and a phone call warned, "If Serena is not returned to the Giubergias the streets will run with blood." Aha, people said. Here's what these emotional outbursts, these wild, uncontrolled feelings lead to: anonymous letters, bombs, threats of slaughter. In truth, *Heart and Tears Italy*, the so-called *Big Mama Italy*, is quite remote from anonymous letters and threats of slaughter. The anonymous letters and threats and the luckily undetonated bomb came from a third Italy, which doesn't heed emotional impulses in the least, but rather pursues its own dark designs, cultivating its goal of terror, discrediting everyone and polluting the atmosphere.

I wrote three newspaper articles on the Serena Cruz case. Many others like myself also wrote about it, people who had no legal background but were expressing their personal views. We were seen as educated people, but lacking any legal training. That is certainly true in my case. I have no legal background whatsoever. Since we were venturing into unfamiliar territory, we were said to be creating confusion and disorder. And yet any casual passerby, without legal training, shouts out loud if he sees something patently unjust taking place. He is not creating confusion, simply shouting in protest. He hopes help will arrive from somewhere. That is why he shouts.

Each time one of my three articles appeared, I received severely disapproving letters, letters that referred to the Giubergias with keen hostility, indeed with harsh acrimony. They spoke of their great selfishness. "They already have a boy, and they wanted a little girl too, eh?" Many people see adoption as an act of selfishness, of greedy, predatory appropriation. As if bringing up a child is a lark. It may be a wonderful thing but it is not a lark. It is wonderful and can bring happiness. But it is no lark. It exacts a price of sleep, worries, fears, labor and self-sacrifice. It is far more convenient to live without children. Anyone who sees people who wish to adopt a child as rapacious and voracious birds of prey has evidently never known or has forgotten all the labor and anguish it takes to raise a child.

Because I wrote articles on the Serena Cruz affair, I happened to be invited to participate in conferences on this case and on adoption in general. I participated several times. To tell the truth, Serena Cruz was very seldom discussed at these conferences, if at all. I always had the sense that the speakers were using a totally unreal language. Not only the Serena Cruz case, but the idea of children in general, living, breathing children with real and individual destinies, seemed very far from these gatherings. They were conferences of speechifiers, each one focused on his own speech and how long it would last. For professional speakers, the length of a speech is critical: for quite a long time, they can be the center of attention, even the center of the world, in a way. Often a speaker will forget the meaning and purpose of his speech because he's so entranced with the sound of his own voice, the fluidity of his language, and his own grandeur in the role of speaker.

Later on I read a book by Oliver Sacks, *The Man Who Mistook His Wife for a Hat.* The first essay, from which the title of the collection is taken, relates the case of Doctor P., a musician and music teacher who consulted the doctor because of various problems with vision and memory. He responded to the doctor's questions in a strange way. He was shown a rose and asked what it was. He answered: "About six inches in length. A convoluted red form with a linear green attachment." He was shown a glove and asked what it was. He answered: "A continuous surface, enfolded on itself. It appears to have five outpouchings, if this is the word." Just as he was going out, Doctor P. "started to look around for his hat. He reached out his hand and took hold of his wife's head, tried to lift it off, to put it on. He had apparently mistaken his wife for a hat!"

Doctor P. was detached from the real world and dwelt in a world of visual abstractions rather than reality. There was no longer any difference, in his eyes, between his wife's head and his hat.

Doctor P.'s language reminded me of the language spoken at those conferences on adoption. In that language, too, there were no more roses or gloves, and in their place were wordy arguments and verbal constructs; the difference between living beings and inanimate objects, between human heads and hats, had vanished.

During those conferences on adoption, I had the definite feeling that the ones who were raving mad—not only on the subject of Serena Cruz but on every circumstance related to adoption in general, or to family feeling, paternity and maternity—were not those labeled "heart and tears Italy," but, on the contrary, the social workers and their colleagues in the various social work agencies, and the world of the juvenile court judges in general. Raving and unreal.

"Don't lynch those judges," many people wrote, explaining that the court had acted with deep and subtle legal understanding in the Serena Cruz affair, risking public opprobrium and demonstrating great courage and dedication to duty. But in considering a judge's decision, I think one should not dwell too much on the subtlety of his legal understanding, or better still, not examine his decision exclusively from that perspective. One should ask solely whether it did or did not serve the goal of justice. We need not even consider whether he was cowardly or brave. Certainly courage is needed to face unpopularity, disapproval, and widespread anger. No doubt in other circumstances, judicial courage can be admirable. But it is admirable when it is exercised in the cause of justice. In the quest for justice, and in its light, courage makes sense. In this particular instance, it was not important to demonstrate courage; what was required was sensitivity and understanding.

The spectacle of courage in other judges has been admirable and splendid because it was used in the service of truth and justice, sometimes even at the risk of their lives.

It is true that the juvenile court judges received anonymous death threats. They have had to face down unpopularity. They have had to confront public indignation. Surely that must have made them acutely uncomfortable. But their judicial pride and obstinacy were more pressing than their discomfort. They probably put little stock in the anonymous letters and threats. They felt strength in numbers. They also enjoyed the support of a large part of the country, that part they called *Rational Italy*. That was the Italy they felt merited their respect. The others, they saw as just so much scum.

As far as their dedication to duty, I cannot forget that in all the fourteen months that Serena Cruz was living in Racconigi with the parents they deemed illegal, the judges never felt the need to go to see her even once. I have said it before, but I will say it again. All they had to do was get on a train. A mere train ride. Not one of them ever thought that since her fate was at stake, he ought to take this little train ride in order to understand, to see the child in the setting of that house and family. From their faraway desks, they decreed that she must be removed. When asked why they never went to see her, they gave no answer. Others answered for them: it was not incumbent upon them to do so. Someone pointed out to me that that is correct. Such an action is not legally required of judges. In the first place, it is wrong not to require it. Furthermore, legal requirements aside, how is it possible, in this case, that not one of them felt the need to go?

Still, no one in the world should be lynched, obviously. Besides, it is not known whether in this case, or in similar cases that have since come to light, the judges' decision was unanimous; it may well be that some of them wanted, or still want, a different outcome.

What is more, we have the feeling that the judges are burdened by a mentality that goes far beyond the realm of the juvenile court, even beyond the realm of government agencies altogether—a mentality that pervades all of society today. A mentality that fears emotion, that fears "heart and tears" in particular, as if they were something filthy that could soil the body. It fears them powerfully; it distrusts them. It honors and respects only what is controlled, disciplined, and lukewarm. We have become a society of the lukewarm, of those "neither cold nor hot."

I am by no means suggesting that all the juvenile court judges are like this. Nor are all the people who supported them in the Serena Cruz case. Some are moved by a different idea, by their faith in the law, which is not lukewarm.

Still, a lukewarm mentality permeates our society: we can feel it in the air around us. It speaks a cunning, studied, falsely rational language, the language of pseudoscience. It cloaks itself in false scientific knowledge, false because poorly understood and poorly assimilated, lacking any firm foundation. It claims to know all sorts of things others know nothing about. It fears and rejects the coldness of true science, and fears and rejects still more the heat of emotional identification. It takes pride in itself and usually triumphs. Its language prevails. Its wordy and interminable discussions prevail. They are well-bred discussions, controlled in tone, disciplined, tepid, and amenable to all that is tepid. We find them in the press, in conversation, in debates, meetings, and panel discussions. Such a mentality, always proudly cloaked in its tepid, falsely scientific, pedagogical and sociological lore, is prone to drift off into abstraction. We watch it settle there, far above the stumbling blocks, in its own arrogant lukewarmness, seemingly safe, as if nothing could chill or threaten or stain or sully it. Its wordy arguments sound totally removed from reality. In truth, if we listen carefully, without allowing ourselves to be carried away by their well-bred, lukewarm flow, they sound quite mad. Raving mad, as mad as the words of the man who mistook his wife for his hat.

Thus we have a marriage of the lukewarm and the delirious. A delirious lukewarmness and a lukewarm delirium. This most bizarre coupling dominates our public discourse. I cannot say for certain, but I suspect there has never been anything quite like it before.

In the Serena Cruz case, this mentality rooted in abstractions naturally and without hesitation chose the millions of abstract children and was indifferent to the fate of a single very visible, living child; it applauded the court's decision.

This kind of mentality has no love for the spirit of sacrifice: it is too generous. This mentality distrusts and rejects generosity. In place of the word "generosity" it prefers to use the word "altruism," which is more technical and hence more staid, dignified, lukewarm, and unemotional. It prefers a love that is tepid, parsimonious, controlled, and disciplined. So controlled and so disciplined that it is hardly love at all. Such a mentality cannot possibly comprehend the Giubergias: awkward, maladroit, ingenuous, generous, passionate, and quite unable to respond to those accusing them of a crime. You already adopted one child, they were told, so you must have been aware of the long and laborious process. But maybe they thought telling a lie to the authorities was not the end of the world. They were in a hurry, so they broke the law. That's what I think might have happened. Assuming what the judges say is true, that is, and they really did lie.

They offered the child their love and their labor; they made sacrifices for her. They taught her not to look for food in bags of garbage and to sleep in a bed. She had nightmares and phobias; they did what they could to reassure her. They were not rich; they gave all they could to bring her up well. They fostered a close relationship with their two children, one legally adopted and the other illegally, a relationship good for all four of them. Was their love "anxiety-producing?" Maybe so, but even an "anxiety-producing" love can bring happiness.

This is what the lukewarm mentality failed to grasp. It is a repressed mentality, yet when it leaves off its wordy arguments it can be crude and cut to the quick. When it leaves off its genteel and wordy arguments, it can make things very simple. "This child will be placed in a new family. Nothing has happened. Everything's fine." As if love were as common and plentiful as grass....

A long article about Serena appeared in *La Stampa* last fall. Over the summer, the press had dropped the matter. From the moment Rosanna Giubergia left her in the local shelter, nothing more was heard of her. She became one of the *desaparecidas*. It was known that they took her away, at night, to another community shelter. But where? Surely she must have been shielded from reporters and curious onlookers. Everyone knew her face—it had been all over the papers for months: her round face, snub nose, wide bewildered eyes, and black bangs. Certainly. But how can a child be shielded from prying eyes? A child has to be taken out for a walk. She can hardly be held prisoner between four walls. So? Did they take her out for a walk or not? How come no one ever happened to meet up with her in some public park, or along the street?

Over the summer, there were conflicting rumors. She was still in that community shelter. No, she was in another one, far from Piedmont, maybe in the South. No, she was in a small group home, ten or fifteen children with caregivers. No, she was already with new parents in pre-adoption. No, no couple would take her because she posed too many problems. Too great a responsibility. Such a famous child. A child who had been all over the papers. A child who had been in the eye of a storm. Besides, she still kept the name of her first adoptive parents. She bears it even today. The Giubergias have not disclaimed her and have no intention of doing so. They still hope she will be returned to them.

Then in the fall that long article appeared. It was all smiles. "Serena's Smiles" was the headline. After so long a silence, the matter resurfaced decked out in its Sunday best. The article seemed written in order to demonstrate the wisdom and virtue of the court's decision. Actually, after so long a silence, some brief notice would have sufficed, preferably skeptical, since anything is conceivable, especially in such a controversial case. "Serena is in a new family now, and seems to be doing well. Or well enough." That might ring true. Instead, the article rang false. Its tone was triumphant. It was dripping with optimism and smugness, buzzing with endless details. Serena is in a pre-adoption phase with new parents. She was taken on vacation to the seashore, they taught her to swim, she has two sisters and a brother, she has lots of toys, red, yellow and green ninepins (the toys were described at length), she fits in perfectly with her new family. She's thrilled to have visitors, gives everyone a big hug. She takes the reporter by the hand. "Come see the starry sky." Does a three-year-old really talk that way? Invite reporters to see the starry sky? Possibly. Paper cutouts of the moon and stars are pasted on the ceiling of a room. In the garden are flower beds, fruit trees, a plastic swimming pool. In the distance, the country landscape. Everything is lovely, everything is calm, bathed in a blissful light. The article says the new adoptive parents are called Papa Franco and Mama Luisa. "We've had lots of help from the court, the social workers, the court-appointed guardian," they say. "Someone comes every day and spends hours. That's probably why it's all gone so smoothly." Strange that the social workers, the guardian, and the court all suddenly roused themselves. For the Giubergias, no one moved a muscle. Now all of a sudden everyone got on the train, the train they couldn't manage to board before. They spend long hours there every day. Papa Franco: "In all these months Serena has never mentioned the past, or the family she lived with when she first arrived in Italy.... We have no objection to having Serena meet with the Giubergias and her big brother, Nazario... but this can take place only when and if the guardian and the psychologists say so.... The Giubergias know where Serena is and how she's doing. They've been kept informed by the court-appointed guardian who comes every day...." Mama Luisa: "We take her out with us every day. We go to the market, do the shopping, often to a restaurant..."

In fact the Giubergias do not know where Serena is. No one has told them anything, they say.

Along with the article was a drawing said to be by Serena Cruz. It could have been done by any child. The caption read:

"The child's fears are over." Serena supposedly showed the reporter her drawing: "Look, this is the Mommy." The drawing showed a crowd of figures, some roundish, some angular. It would be hard to single out a mother. Also hard to single out the vanished fears.

With regard to the Giubergias, the article sounded insulting. Between the lines it seemed to be saying: "You people didn't do right by her, but now our bountiful social agencies have put her in Paradise."

The bountiful social agencies treated the Giubergias like dogs. They hounded and humiliated them and shoved them out of the way. Couldn't they have let them see the child again, at least once? "You have another child," they were told. "That's enough. Now get out of the way." Nazario, their other child, has suffered bitterly over his sister's disappearance. The judges say that sorrows, separations, and losses are healed by the "plasticity of his age." But this "plasticity" exists only in their pronouncements. Why must two children pay for the errors of adults? That question goes unanswered.

Regardless of the article that so amply and triumphantly portrays her in her new family, in the eyes of the people, Serena remains a *desaparecida*. Do these new parents, Papa Franco and Mama Luisa, really exist? People wonder. They may be wrong to wonder, but they do. Could they have been fabricated? Seaside vacations are mentioned, beaches and restaurants. Then why has no one ever caught sight of her, such a well-known child? How do they shield her from curiosity-seekers, or from journalists, who are everywhere?

Let us hope that the article is true at least in some sense. Let us hope that Serena finds herself with understanding people who love her. And let's hope she's not still shut up in an institution, as many people believe.

Some say that by this point, nothing more can be done for her; she is destroyed forever. Others still hope she might return to Racconigi, where the Giubergias keep waiting for her. I believe that were she to return, the Giubergias' enormous happiness would spill over and make her happy too. Her brother would also be happy. If the welfare of the child comes first, why not consider Nazario, too? Isn't he a child as well, a child who saw a happy era of his life destroyed with no plausible explanation, who saw his sister and daily companion vanish overnight, his parents devastated as if someone had died, and yet he knew no one had died? At this point I cannot tell if there is any real basis for hope. In terms of justice, though, true justice, the matter appears by now to be a lost cause.

Some say, why take the destiny of this child so much to heart? There are plenty of children like her, who have been taken from their parents by the authorities and whom no one knows about because there was no press coverage. "Thousands Like Serena," one headline ran. This is quite true. However, it is not the proper way to think about a misfortune. It means diverting your gaze from reality and diffusing it by contemplating an immense, anonymous series of similar cases all over the world, and in effect no longer seeing anything. The sheer size and impact of the numbers crush and eventually bury the details and features of one single, solitary calamity. On the contrary, whenever we witness one person or group of people suffer a misfortune or injustice, our indignation should be felt specifically on their behalf, and should remain vivid in our memory along with the specific details of their misfortune and injustice: indestructible, unique, unlike any other. Serena Cruz must not be forgotten, even if from now on her name need never again be mentioned in the press.

The magistrates complained a good deal about the media uproar. "Stop all that racket. The child has the right to be left in peace." Yes, that would suit you all too well, my esteemed magistrates. The child had many other vital and essential rights, which were stubbornly and ruthlessly trampled on.

People don't trust the public agencies. They used to trust them in matters of adoption and children. They thought they were acting for the public good. Now their trust is gone. They fear them. And so when a sudden silence descended on Serena Cruz, when the whole affair was veiled in secrecy, they saw her as a *desaparecida*, even if it seemed appropriate to protect her with silence. For there is something sinister about bureaucratic silence and secrecy. Everyone recalled the word *desaparecida*, a word of sad memory.

It has since come to light that nobody actually heeds the rule laid down by Cory Aquino, requiring anyone planning to adopt a baby in the Philippines to establish residency there for eighteen months. But the Giubergias must have thought they had to obey it to the letter. So perhaps to avoid breaking one law, they stumbled over another, more serious one—assuming, again, that the judges' and the media's version of the case is the truth.

If that is so, most likely they were poorly advised. The poor are poorly advised. Had they been rich, they would have had plenty of good advice. Had they been intellectuals, they would have used the language of intellectuals—fluent, unconstrained, respected—when responding to the court later on. And they would have known how to speak the language of the lukewarm, the aseptic, disciplined, controlled, and verbose language that prevails nowadays, the language we so often hear spoken in conferences, debates, and panel discussions.

III

This is not an essay on adoption, nor does it make the slightest claim to be. It is merely a series of notes on various matters that came to mind in connection with Serena Cruz, the Giubergias, and other events alluded to in the press that are in some way related to the Serena Cruz case. I began making notes early in October; now it is December. In October I hadn't met the Giubergias. I hadn't even seen them on television, where I know they appeared once. Someone who knew them slightly had told me about them. But I didn't know them and had never taken the train to go and meet them. Since I am not a magistrate, I had no obligation to get on the train, but because I was writing about them, trying to envision them in my mind, I felt I ought to meet them, and felt guilty for not having done so. And so toward the end of November I got on the train (I live in Rome) and went to Turin, then drove to Racconigi in the afternoon with three friends, who also had never met the Giubergias.

The Giubergias are unusual and admirable people. This was my impression. I found them quite similar to what I had imagined, only better, because I hadn't envisioned their strength of heart or their good sense or their great patience. However, I didn't learn much more from them than I already knew. They told me little or nothing about Serena in her own country, or about Francesco Giubergia's second trip there. For my part, I asked very little, out of awkwardness or discretion. I understand and respect their reserve. It stands to reason that they should be reserved with strangers on so delicate a subject. And I was a stranger. An outsider who was on their side, but an outsider nonetheless.

They have spent and continue to spend all their savings on lawyers, in an effort to have the child restored to them; they aren't resigned to losing her. You can find consolation after a death, they say, but for a loss like this there is no possible consolation. They loved her like their own flesh and blood. They wait patiently for her to be returned. Just the other day they heard about a couple whose adopted Peruvian daughter had been taken away, like theirs, on a charge of illegality. After nine months she was given back. Couldn't the same thing happen to them?

Is it impossible? A mad, wild, absurd hope? But hope is mad only when there has been no inhumane act to begin with. If there has been an inhumane act, it isn't mad to hope it will be reversed. It shows faith that in the end, people may prove to be better and more just than they first appeared.

The court has told the Giubergias they will never have Serena back again. Go ahead and adopt other children, they told them, but you will never have Serena again. Meaning that they are worthy of adopting other children but not this child? That's certainly something to puzzle over, day in and day out.

They loved her like their own flesh and blood. What does it matter if she wasn't? They're very concerned about her health. She had problems, she had perforated eardrums. She needed a lot of care. Who knows if she's getting the care she needs? They had seen to all the various vaccinations, they still have all the certificates, yet when she was taken away, no one thought to ask if she had been vaccinated. Nobody even mentioned it. It may seem an irrelevant detail, but it's a sure sign of carelessness. Not even to ask whether or not she was vaccinated?

They show me a court document dated last June. As in the *Stampa* article of September, it describes Serena in her new family. So we have to assume this new family really exists. The name *Serena Cruz* appears at the end of the document, but elsewhere she is called "Chicca." They wanted to take away her true name, just as in the community shelter they immediately took away her earrings and necklace. The report is quite detailed. "Chicca," it says, fits happily into her new family. Nevertheless, between the lines one senses a vague astonishment that she never makes the slightest reference to the past. The world she left behind seems two-dimensional. After reading the report, just as after reading the article, I have the sensation of having wandered through a stage setting, where something is concealed, not only the names and places but something equally crucial....

The whole time I was at their house, Nazario stayed close to his mother. Our presence troubled him. I think he was remembering the visits of the social workers who sat in the kitchen drinking coffee, then took his sister away. He is a frightened child. He went to nursery school for three weeks, then didn't want to go anymore for fear that someone would carry him off, far from his family, as happened to his sister. Upstairs, in the room where he and his sister used to sleep, are two small wooden beds with railings. But he didn't want to sleep up there anymore and now all three, parents and child, sleep downstairs. The house is quiet, low-roofed, surrounded by fields, a house that seems made for children to grow up in peacefully. Everyone in town knows and loves the Giubergias; everyone shared in their great calamity. Whatever aversion and hostility were expressed elsewhere, here in their own town they were helped and sustained by the friendship and solidarity of their neighbors.

In the kitchen are albums of photographs from Manila, of the hotel where they brought Nazario when he was seven months old, so weak and sick that he couldn't eat, and where his adoptive mother spent hours trying to make him swallow a few morsels of food. The hotel was air-conditioned, which he wasn't used to and couldn't tolerate; he immediately developed a high fever. They had to turn it off. They had been told that in order to be found fit to adopt, it would be best to stay in an upscale hotel, and Rosanna Giubergia was also advised to change her outfits often. Rich people are given preference in adoptions. In the last photos, taken shortly before they returned to Italy, when Nazario had been with them for two months, he already looks like a healthy baby.

There is a large photo of Serena taken during her last days in Racconigi, a photo I had seen in the papers earlier. What a happy face! "Fourteen months of violence in Racconigi," the president of ANFAA [National Association of Adoptive and Foster Care Families] allegedly said at a conference in Rimini. Does the president of ANFAA know what the word "violence" means? Could he really have said that, as reported? Should someone for whom words have lost their true meaning be permitted to make public statements? For anyone with any grasp of reality, of the kind of life Serena led with her parents in Racconigi, don't those words take on the accents of madness? Could this be *Rational Italy*?

IV

...In dealing with children, the judicial system can move with lightning speed; then again, when speed is required, it moves at the pace of a caterpillar. In the Serena Cruz case, with the court already suspecting some illegality when the child had been in Italy just a few days, a swift resolution was essential. But it was only a suspicion, they say. And so months and months went by. When the machinery was finally set in motion, it moved like lightning, heedless of anything in its path. If they intended to take action, shouldn't they have done so before such a strong and deep bond had developed between the child and the Giubergias? The bureaucratic suspicion lasted fourteen months. Then they made up their minds in barely more than a day, and their decision was lightning swift, lacerating, and merciless....

Those working in the field of adoption maintain that a child must be given a family, and not, as before, that a family must be given a child. On this we can all agree.

The interests of the child, the well-being of the child, must be at the heart of every choice and determination.

Give a family to a child and not a child to a family. Obviously. However, when a child is adopted, his destiny is at once linked to the destiny of those who adopt him. If they love him and are happy with him, then the child is happy with them too. Well-being, in its universal and actual sense, meaning harmony and mutual understanding, cannot help but be mutual. Once the adoption takes place, the child and the family become one unit. So if one really thinks about it, that seemingly very obvious sentence makes no sense at all.

After the Serena Cruz affair, we would often find stories in the papers about children taken away from their parents, both adoptive and biological. Stories of children carried off from home or school or day-care centers by social workers and police under court orders, and put up for adoption. The judges then select whichever new families they please. The parents will lose the children forever, never see them again. In some cases it's not a question of parents, adoptive or biological, but of grandparents or aunts or uncles who have raised the children because they were orphaned. The specific grounds given by the court vary with each case. The family's poverty or misfortune. An illegality in the adoption, in cases of adoption. The grandparents' advanced age. The aunts' and uncles' precarious health. So nowadays anyone who is poor must live with yet another terror: their children may be taken away. The same goes for anyone old or sick. But the way the child is carried off is generally the same—social workers and police. And the basic justification is always the same: the well-being of the child. The child's life is destroyed so as to rebuild it better. Better, that is, as the bureaucracy interprets it. But in the meantime it must be destroyed. These days we know all too well that childhood trauma begets irreparable consequences. Everyone knows that. It is common knowledge. And still the traumas continue, inexorably, with the force of law behind them....

Parents and relatives protest in every possible way when their children are taken away. Very often neighbors, friends or concerned strangers protest along with them. Committees are formed, letters go off to the Pope, the President of the Republic, the Attorney General. But usually all in vain. The magistrates in charge of child welfare do not usually reverse themselves. Their will is irrevocable, their decisions written in stone. For a few days, sometimes for months, the papers report the parents' despair and the indignation of the citizenry, at least of those citizens who find such acts outrageous and inhuman. Then comes silence. The various committees give up and gradually disband. What is to be done? From then on, no one knows what happens to the children. No one hears anymore about them. They vanish into institutions and the Juvenile Court puts them up for adoption. Are they actually adopted or placed in foster families, or do they stay in institutions for years on end? No one ever knows. Only the authorities know. And how can people trust the authorities? They have no more trust. After so many strange and cruel incidents, how can people still believe that the authorities really trouble themselves about *the welfare of the child?*

What is genuinely good for a child is to grow up with someone who loves him. This may not be the same thing as his *well-being,* but it is his good. Well-being, material well-being, can vanish overnight and leave no trace. But good stays rooted. To uproot and destroy it can leave a child miserable for the rest of his life. To the end of his days he will harbor the memory, conscious or unconscious, of the day his home and family, everything he thought he possessed, disappeared in a flash.

What is good for a child is to be brought up by someone for whom he is of supreme value. Children who grow up in institutions can sense that they are not of supreme value for anyone in the world.

But love in and of itself may not always be good, the psychologists say: it might be an unhealthy, oppressive, or obsessive kind of love. Yes, but it is still love. The nature of love can be misleading. A love that seems calm and stable one day can become oppressive the next. Meanwhile it is still love. No one can predict the future. But for today, grant a child what she needs today. Today she needs to grow up with a person or persons for whom she is of supreme value. If she is growing up this way, let her be. No one should be allowed to interfere with her....

What should public agencies do? It is so simple and so obvious that it shouldn't need to be spelled out. If the family breadwinner is unemployed, they should help him or her find work. If the family is homeless, they should find them a home. If the children are being raised by old grandparents, they should get help for the grandparents and the children. If the children are not properly washed or dressed, if they have lice, the social workers should take the trouble to bring them clothes and ointments and see that they are kept clean. Otherwise why have social workers at all? What purpose do they serve?

Or is the job of the social worker merely to submit his suitably wordy reports to the courts, reports that contain not the slightest awareness of real life and real people?

Does the government of a civilized country behave this way? Send police into people's homes? Make children vanish into thin air?

The citizens make up the State. It is their absolute right to be assisted by the State when they are in dire need. It is the State's strict duty to come to their aid. It does not do so. It should, but it doesn't. Instead it grinds families to bits. It separates children from parents. Brothers from brothers. What must we think of such a State? What kind of trust can we place in it?

Only in the most extreme circumstances should children be taken away from the people who are raising them. When those people are doing them harm—tangible, actual, obvious harm. When a child shows real and evident signs of disturbance or pain or depravity in the family, or signs of abuse or mistreatment. When it is impossible to resolve a terrible situation except by separation. Then it is a matter beyond any help. Only then does the State have the right to intervene. Otherwise, every intervention of the State is violent and unjust; indeed, any intervention of the State into people's private lives without valid justification is violent and unjust....

The authorities responsible for children have lost the acuity that distinguishes one act from another and grasps the diversity of human traits and human situations; they have lost the vision that rises from deep within and seeks to comprehend what is good and what is evil. In its place is an abstract idea of perfection. An aseptic, rarefied idea. The authorities proceed with this idea raised aloft before them like a banner. And so they take children away from the poor, or the old, from those who raise them and love them, raising and loving them as best they can, with difficulty and privation, maybe in a disorderly way, not according to the rules in the manuals. *The best interests of the child* must be protected, they say. But in truth it is not possible to protect the best interests of the child or of anyone else, if the vision that distinguishes good from evil is extinguished, and in its place stands an abstract, aseptic, rarefied idea of perfection, conscious only of itself and its own rigid standards....

What is a family? It is the focal point where a group of people come together, whether in a house or a room or a trailer. They form bonds—strong or weak, fleeting or tenacious. From this point, a child views the rest of the world.

Families may be terrible, repressive, obsessive; or indifferent, or estranged, or inattentive; or poisonous, corrupt, rotten— they very often are. But children need them. You cannot pluck a child out of one family and plant him in another except for extremely serious reasons. Even so, it will devastate his spirit. He may be growing up wretched, be ashamed of his family and hate it; still, this is a wretchedness his memory can feed on, thickening day by day. In future days, he can lead his memory through the thickets of that dense forest. Changing a child's environment is injurious. He has to view the world from a new point. The old point of view and the new one clash. War breaks out. This kind of war can be worse than wretchedness: later on, memory will look back over that wasteland and search fruitlessly for the remains of the childhood that once was....

When a woman adopts a child, there quickly develops a relationship just like a blood tie. How this happens is hard to explain. And yet it happens. She didn't carry him in her own body, didn't give birth to him. But she knows she is the point from which he will come to view the world.

She also knows that he knows he is of supreme value to her. And once this has happened, we must leave them in peace. If problems or complications arise, we must bend over backwards to see that they are left in peace.

There is no great difference between the maternal and paternal instincts. In men, the paternal instinct may arise more slowly and be accompanied by more ideas. In women, the maternal instinct arises and flourishes mute, without ideas. Quite often the roles and instincts become blurred. Within every man is a woman and within every woman, a man. There is only one real difference between men and women, and that one is immense. Women bear children. This is why there arises between a woman and an adopted child, born of another woman, that subterranean, dark, damp and tortuous connection that binds mothers and children and seems to carry with it distant memories no one else can penetrate....

I heard about a couple, some time ago, who couldn't have children and applied to adopt a baby. Both husband and wife were questioned, subjected to the customary long and grueling investigation. The woman went home in tears. The interrogation was severe, arduous, and exceedingly unpleasant. In the end, they were found unfit to adopt. According to their interrogators, the couple "had no imagination," and therefore were unable to raise a child in the best possible manner. They had been asked if they liked to travel. They both responded that they had no great interest in traveling. They were two unassuming office workers without much money for unnecessary expenses. For this reason, their "lack of imagination," they were rejected. A few years later they adopted a Peruvian girl.

I recount this story because I find it illuminating. Whoever examined that couple is ideologically under the sway not only of an abstract concept of perfection, but also of wholly artificial and distorted notions regarding imagination and travel, notions of a profound and abysmal imbecility. If that couple could truly love a child and make her happy—a child who would otherwise face God knows what kind of life simply because they said they don't like to travel—then obviously that distorted vision of the world is terribly inauspicious. It reveals a worldview that is itself abstract, a view in which the words "imagination" and "travel" have taken on a meaning totally unrelated to their actual meaning. This kind of worldview, patching together a

smattering of poorly understood and poorly assimilated notions derived from pseudoscience, is dangerous and ill-omened
precisely because it is so self-satisfied and sure of its own power;
aggressive and bullying, it is generally validated, indeed enthu-
siastically applauded, by society at large. Pseudoscience is prop-
agated everywhere and for the most part is greeted with
enthusiasm. It takes considerable effort to perceive that behind
it is the void.

V

...We have the sense that the Juvenile Court's power in the field
of adoption grows more blind, more deaf, and more isolated
every day. No outside voices reach them, not the voices of the
highest authorities nor those of the people. The bridges between
the Juvenile Court judges and the people have collapsed. And
thus the bridges between the Juvenile Court judges and justice itself have also collapsed. For if the people demand what is humane
and just and get no response, where then can justice be sought?

We have the sense that the world of adoption is ruled by an
abstract idea of perfection conjoined with chaos.

To maintain this abstract idea of perfection, specters must be
conjured up. To be sure, specters do exist, and very real ones:
children are abused, raped, bought and sold; children are
adopted for God knows what reasons; children are used to sell
drugs or for other criminal dealings. And yet specters are no
proper foundation for legal proceedings, or for managing any
aspect of daily reality, or reality as a whole.

The social workers and child welfare agencies have a share in
the court's supreme authority; they support it and take pride in
its foresight and perspicacity. And they in turn exert the same
power, bringing to it a mentality utterly detached from the real
world and from ordinary people: a mentality made up of words

glued together by pseudoscience. A lukewarm mentality. The lukewarmness, as I have said, comes from the rejection of the coldness of true science and the rejection of the warmth of emotional identification. From this double rejection, the tribe of the tepid is born. Tepidness and abstraction wheel about together in chaos. What was once commonly called "good will" or "human decency" has fallen into total discredit and is viewed with scorn and disgust by a vast segment of society, and consequently by the world of child welfare. Obviously "good intentions" and "human decency" deserve scorn when they are feigned but not when they are genuine. And among the good intentions that may indeed be genuine are a handful of precious and irreplaceable blessings such as understanding, tolerance and compassion, and the ability to contemplate every human face and every human situation by its own light and in its own singularity. In the world of child welfare, all the lights are out. It moves in darkness.

People in the street gaze wide-eyed, in shock and dismay, at this world immersed in darkness. They raise their voices in anger and protest, but their cries go unheeded.

What the Serena Cruz case has shown us, over and above the issue of how the law is to be enforced, is how very tragic our loss of those precious and irreplaceable blessings has become.

Some people want to see the Juvenile Court abolished and its functions assigned to specific branches of the ordinary courts. That is the system in other countries. I am not sure. I tend to think that questions of child care and protection and all the choices involved therein are so delicate, so tangled with emotion, and so complex that a branch of the judicial system needs to be devoted exclusively and intensely to their consideration. But one thing is certain: social workers, juvenile court judges, everyone presently involved in the world of child welfare should, if not disappear entirely, then be utterly transformed....

On the other hand, here is Alessandro Galante Garrone's opinion (*La Stampa*, May 6, 1989):

"Enforce the existing laws: what else must judges all over the world do? This is a universal principle of the modern era which has prevailed since the Age of Enlightenment and the French Revolution.... I am reminded of something Salvemini* liked to quote—a great American Supreme Court Justice's sharp reprimand to the lawyer who was invoking justice: 'I am not here to dispense justice but to enforce the law.'"

With all due respect to Galante Garrone, to the memory of Salvemini, and to that great American Supreme Court Justice, I must say that I do not understand these words. They may be legally unexceptionable, but to me they make no sense. To me, justice and the law must be one and the same. I know quite well how often they are not; nevertheless they ought to be. How can we conceive of them as separate? Are laws not made to uphold justice? To uphold the rights of the weaker against the stronger?

If not, why have laws at all? What purpose do they serve?

And if on occasion justice and law clearly diverge, if a law turns out to be flawed or deficient, then shouldn't the magistrates make superhuman efforts to enforce it as fairly as possible? Especially when the rights and destiny of a child are at stake? Or else resign from office if they cannot succeed?

Can anything be more crucial than justice, in governing nations, in responding to human situations and human needs? No. Nothing in the world can take precedence over justice.

December, 1989

---

* Gaetano Salvemini, early-20th-century writer on politics and political philosophy.

acknowledgments

M y deepest thanks to Marco Praderio and Daniele Scalise for their generous and invaluable help with certain mysteries of Italian, to Carl Phillips for elucidating the Latin phrases and references, and to Lisa Ronchi and Vittorio Nuti for information on the Serena Cruz case. Thanks also to the National Endowment for the Arts for their generous support of this project.

source materials

The material in *A Place to Live* was drawn from:

Le piccole virtú, Giulio Einaudi Editore, 1962
Mai devi domandarmi, Aldo Garzanti Editore, 1970
Vita immaginaria, Arnoldo Mondadori Editore, 1974
Serena Cruz o la vera giustizia, Giulio Einaudi Editore, 1990